...MA

...ANDS

WEST INDIES

Caicos Passage

Caicos Islands

Turks Islands

...d Passage

I.Tortue

C.FRANCES

St NICOLAS

HAITI

SAN DOMINGO

SANTO DOMINGO

PUERTO RICO

Virgin Islands

LESSER

St Kitts

Nevis

Antigua

Guadeloupe

LEEWARD ISLANDS

Dominica

ANTILLES

St PIERRE

Martinique

St Lucia

...NTILLES

St Vincent

Barbados

WINDWARD ISLANDS

Grenada

...EAN   SEA

Tobago

TRINIDAD

...DA

VENEZUELA

...TH   AMERICA

500	250	0

Scale in Miles

Three Brothers at Havana
1762

For Wacky and Lucy

Three Brothers
at Havana
1762

Sonia Keppel

Michael Russell

© Sonia Keppel 1981

First published in Great Britain 1981 by
Michael Russell (Publishing) Ltd.,
The Chantry, Wilton, Salisbury, Wiltshire

Indexes and Glossary by P. S. H. Lawrence

Printed in Great Britain by
Biddles Ltd., Guildford, Surrey

Contents

List of Illustrations

I

'England on Board Her Fleet'

As far back as 1741, at the outbreak of the War of the Austrian Succession, William Pitt had made no secret of his conviction that, to conquer France, England's first duty was to beat her at sea and isolate her from her colonial possessions. For him, George II's obsession with the preservation of his electorate of Hanover and consequent German alliance came as a bad second. His attitude infuriated the King who for a long time would not tolerate him in his Government. But by 1756 the country's need and its clamour for Pitt to lead it in its hour of crisis established him at its head, and by 1757 his grand project of 'putting England on board her fleet' was under way.

Thanks to well-balanced operations between British naval and military units round the world, by 1760 the rout of the French colonial possessions by the British was almost complete. In the East Indies Rear-Admiral Watson and Lieutenant-Colonel Clive had successfully recaptured Calcutta and Chandernagore. In Canada Admiral Boscawen, Major-General Amherst and Brigadier James Wolfe had laid successful siege to Louisbourg, thereby giving the British control of all Cap Breton Island and the mouth of the St. Lawrence river. Two years later, Vice-Admiral Saunders helped Wolfe (now a major-general) to storm the Heights of Abraham, to take Quebec and to drive the French from Montreal and the whole of French Canada. On the west coast of Africa British ships captured Senegal and the island of Goree. In the Mediterranean Boscawen's and Hawke's decisive victories effectively snapped the link between France and her possessions overseas. In three years England passed from limited military engagements to worldwide naval victories.

Yet in all this glowing panorama one black spot stood out: England's lost bargaining point in the Mediterranean, her island of Minorca. To right this, Pitt determined to subdue the French island of Belleisle and commissioned a young naval captain, Augustus Keppel, to make a preliminary survey. Despite the strongly fortified coast, Keppel reported that he thought a landing on it could be made. Pitt ordered him to assume command of a squadron of twenty-one ships of the line, with bomb-vessels and fire-ships and, with the rank of commodore, to place himself under the command of Admiral Hawke. The first expedition was prevented from sailing by the death of George II.

The King was succeeded by his grandson, George, Prince of Wales, who was anxious to make peace with France. But Pitt was as determined as ever to achieve his objective, and in the New Year of 1761 his project against Belleisle was resumed.

With Commodore Keppel in command of the squadron and Major-General Studholme Hodgson commanding the land forces, after a strenuous and valorous campaign the sub-jugation of Belleisle was achieved. Thereafter, Pitt increased Keppel's command till it totalled sixty-three ships of the line. With this added strength, he was ordered to patrol the French coast and to keep the French fleet bottled up in Brest harbour. For Pitt realised that, despite her recent reverses, France was as anxious as ever to regain her power at sea; and that to achieve this she would have to bring in Spain.

When in August 1761 a 'Family Compact' between Bourbon France and Bourbon Spain was declared (whereby a fifty–fifty offensive and defensive pact between them was made for the duration of the war), Pitt was not surprised. His struggle to get the King and the Duke of Newcastle's largely pacifist Cabinet to agree to a declaration of war on Spain became increasingly acrimonious and led to his resignation; but not before he had laid his plans to oust France from her remaining foothold in the West Indies, the island of Martinique. In overall command of this project he put Rear-Admiral Rodney. This was the last appointment he made before his resignation.

2

Three Brothers Unite

On 20 November 1761 Viscount Anson, First Lord of the Admiralty, signalled the fleet that an ultimatum had been delivered to Spain through the British Ambassador in Madrid, the Earl of Bristol, demanding to know whether she intended to ally herself with France against England. Should the answer be yes, Lord Bristol was to leave Madrid at once without taking leave and go to Lisbon. He was first to give warning of his action to Rear-Admiral Saunders (in command, Mediterranean fleet) and Commodore Keppel (who was instructed to watch the Spanish port of Cadiz). The Spanish answer was non-committal but on 10 December Spain issued an order to seize all British shipping. On Christmas Eve the news of Spain's belligerency reached England; on 26 December the *Gazette* announced a state of war with Spain.

William, Duke of Cumberland, George III's uncle, had had a chequered career in the army. First acclaimed for his defeat of Charles Edward, the Young Pretender, at Culloden, he soon earned the opprobrious title of 'Butcher' Cumberland for the rigours of his stewardship of the Scottish Highlands. In his campaign in the Low Countries he was out-manoeuvred by Maréchal Saxe and in 1757, after his disastrous capitulation to another French general, d'Estrées, at the Battle of Klosterzeven, he was recalled, humiliated by his father, George II, and obliged to abandon his military career. Even so, he still maintained close contacts with William Pitt in Government, Lord Anson at the Admiralty, and Lord

Ligonier at the War Office, and he was respectfully listened
to by his nephew, George III. As a result, when in January
1762 he submitted a plan to George III's Government for a
secret invasion of Havana, the capital of the Spanish colony
of Cuba, it had from the outset the backing of Pitt, Anson
and Ligonier.

The year before, in the sixth year of the Seven Years' War,
the plan, based on a careful survey by Admiral Knowles, had
already been approved by Pitt. Following the revelation of
the 'Family Compact' between Spain and France, he had
been anxious to seize the rich treasure-ships of Spain before
they reached their depot at Havana. Like Drake in 1585,
he was bent on 'stabbing Spain in the heart of her colonial
power and wealth'. In 1748, during the War of the Austrian
Succession, Admiral Knowles had himself conducted an
abortive operation against Havana. In 1752 he had been appointed Governor of Jamaica, and four years later had been
entertained on a courtesy tour of Havana by the Spanish
Governor of Cuba. While there, he had memorised material
for a detailed report on the defence of Havana together with
its strengths and weaknesses. His conclusions had been that
Havana was a suitable object for assault and that its acquisi-
tion would open up unparalleled advantages to the victors.
As we have seen, Pitt was foiled in his desire to declare war
on Spain by the vacillation of the Duke of Newcastle's government, but his enthusiasm for the Duke of Cumberland's
plan remained unchanged.

Lord Anson put his project to the Secret Committee, called
to finalise the plan of war. The Duke of Newcastle (First
Lord of the Treasury), the Duke of Devonshire, George
Grenville (Treasurer of the Navy) and the two Secretaries of
State, Lord Bute and Lord Egremont, were called to meet
Lord Anson and Lord Ligonier. To quote the Duke of New-
castle: 'We began with my Lord Anson's project of attacking

Havana and, after hearing the facility with which his Lord-ship and Lord Ligonier apprehended there was in doing it, we all unanimously ordered the undertaking.' Hitherto Lord Anson had declared it impossible for the British fleet to under-take a war with France and Spain together, but now he pressed on with this dual purpose, though success was not achieved until after his death.

Feeling that the expedition's supreme commander must be a man of the highest moral fibre and of undisputed talent as a navigator and seaman, and being unable to spare Lord Hawke or Sir Charles Saunders from their vital commands in the Channel and Mediterranean, Anson advanced the name of Admiral of the Blue Sir George Pocock, erstwhile Com-mander-in-Chief East Indies. As his second-in-command he proposed Augustus Keppel, with the rank of commodore, but with a special commission to become Admiral Pocock's successor, in the event of the Admiral's death. Having taken him as lieutenant in *Centurion*, Lord Anson held Keppel in affectionate esteem and the succeeding years had redoubled his faith in Keppel's prowess as a seaman. In 1756 Anson had procured a new ship, *Torbay*, for Augustus Keppel. In this 'seventy-four' he formed part of Admiral Hawke's squadron which had dispersed the French reinforcements gathering in the Basque Roads, destined for Louisbourg on Cap Breton Island. (In this pursuit, though wounded, he had pressed on and taken an enemy ship.) In 1758, in com-mand of a squadron, Keppel chalked up the island of Goree to his credit, following the British capture of Senegal. And in the following year, under Admiral Hawke in Quiberon Bay, his brilliant manoeuvre to sink the French ship *Thésée* was acknowledged as an act of 'superior seamanship'. (As a result of this engagement, naval officers were commissioned in the Marines for the first time, when together Captains Sir Piercy Britt, Viscount Howe and Augustus Keppel were made colonels of the Portsmouth, Plymouth and Chatham Divisions.) Shortly after this, Keppel, complete with officers and crew, was moved to the *Valiant*, a new 'seventy-four'. In this ship he headed the naval command in the attack on the island of Belleisle. To quote the contemporary historian, Thomas Mante:

> This officer had distinguished himself during the whole progress of the [Seven Years'] War. He added Goree (an island on the West coast of Africa) to the British Empire; but his great judgment and activity, so eminently displayed during the recent reduction of Belleisle, was assurance of success to the present enterprise as far as success could be secured by innate bravery, long experience, and great military ability.

Anson's recommendation that Keppel's lieutenant-general brother, George, 3rd Earl of Albemarle, should command the land forces at Havana was less well founded. Although from the age of nineteen he had served on the Duke of Cumberland's staff in all his battles in the Low Countries and at Culloden, Lord Albemarle (unlike his father and grandfather) had never commanded in the field. General Wolfe had dismissed him as a parade officer, '... one of those showy men who are seen in palaces and the courts of men'. But now he had one powerful promoter—the Duke himself.

Since the advent of the young King to the throne, Cumberland had regained much of his former ascendancy. Although no longer holding military office, he was very close to his nephew, and now regularly attended at Court. He had not changed with the years and was still certain that his method of spotting talent in the army was the right one, and that no officer was fit for promotion who had not served on his staff. As he genuinely believed that his 'family' possessed the best military talent in the country, he felt it was his duty to advance its suitability to serve on the secret expedition assembling for Havana. So not only did he nominate Lord Albemarle as Commander-in-Chief, Land Forces; he also approved of the appointment of William Keppel, another of Lord Albemarle's brothers, as one of the two divisional generals; and of the appointment of Colonel Guy Carleton, as Quartermaster-General. All had served on his staff.

Second-in-command to Lord Albemarle was Lieutenant-General George Eliott, a grenadier and a fine soldier, who in 1759 had fought with distinction against the French at Cherbourg and St. Malo, and had since been commanding his regiment in Germany, under Prince Ferdinand of Prussia. Lafausille was William Keppel's opposite number as divisional general. Colonel Guy Carleton had been General Wolfe's favourite officer, and he had recently served with conspicuous gallantry in command of a brigade under Major-General Hodgson at Belleisle.

There were some who said that, with three Keppels appointed to key posts on the forthcoming expedition, undue favouritism was being shown them. But undoubtedly Augustus Keppel was appointed on his own merits. And Lord Ligonier had had personal experience of William Keppel's courage when in 1747 he had charged 'knee to knee' beside him at the Battle of Laffeldt in Flanders, when both were wounded and taken prisoner. Thereafter, Ligonier had watched William Keppel's military progress: his appointment in 1750 as captain in the First Foot Guards; in 1760 to second major with the rank of colonel in the First Foot Guards; in 1761 to the colonelcy of the Fifty-Sixth Foot. For the forthcoming expedition to Havana, he was given the acting rank of major-general, and was Lord Ligonier's special choice to conduct the siege operations against the Moro Castle, the fortress dominating the entrance to the harbour at Havana.

3
The Keppels' Background

The three brothers were the eldest of the five surviving sons of the fifteen children sired by William Anne, 2nd Earl of Albemarle (so named after his godmother, Queen Anne, who had personally sponsored him at his christening) with his wife, also called Anne, daughter of the 1st Duke of Richmond. (Only two daughters had lived of the seven to whom Lady Albemarle had given birth, Lady Caroline and Lady Elizabeth Keppel.) The fourth and fifth sons were Frederick, who became Bishop of Exeter, and Henry, who vanished from the family records after running into debt at Gibraltar, surrendering to the Spanish governor and becoming a Roman Catholic.

Both William Anne and his father, Arnold Joost van Keppel, the first Earl, had been soldiers of note. Arnold, as a young man, had come over from Holland in the train of Stadtholder William and his English wife, Mary, and had later distinguished himself in Marlborough's campaigns. William Anne, already commanding a Guards Brigade in the Low Countries, was recalled to serve under the Duke of Cumberland at Culloden. He succeeded the Duke as Commander-in-Chief of the Forces in Scotland, where his wise and temperate rule did much to ameliorate the conditions of the Scots. He then returned to Flanders, where he was in command of the British infantry under Cumberland, who headed the Confederate army of English, Hanoverian, Hessian, Dutch and Austrian troops against the French. The unequal contest between the Confederate army and the armies led by Maréchal Saxe continued for another year. In April 1748 the Congress of Aix-la-Chapelle was convened, and six months later a definitive treaty was signed, recognising the right of Maria Theresa to the Hapsburg Succession. In recognition of his services to his country, William Anne, Lord Albemarle, was made Governor of Virginia and created a Knight of the Garter. Thereafter, he was appointed ambassador to the Court of France. Diplomatically able but incurably extravagant, he died at Paris of a sudden heart attack in December 1754.

At the time of his marriage (in 1722) to Lady Anne Lennox he had had a fortune of £90,000, to which she had added her dowry of £25,000; but at his death only £14,000 of the original sum remained. And, according to Horace Walpole, purveyor of gossip to his friend at Florence, Sir Horace Mann, despite '£15,000 from government' he had left 'not a shilling to his family, legitimate and illegitimate (both very numerous)'. George II took pity on Lord Albemarle's widow and gave her a pension of £1,200 a year. But when the new peer (George, the third Earl) went to hand back his father's Order of the Garter to his Sovereign, George II greeted him with a homily: 'Your father had a great many good qualities but he was a sieve.'

So, apart from their pay in the Services, the first three Keppel sons were impecunious; and, though unmarried at the time of the Havana campaign, both George and Augustus had illicit families to maintain: George, that of Mrs. Sarah Stanley by whom he already had two children, and Augustus, that of Mrs. Wells, by whom he had a daughter. At that time, William Keppel appears to have been unattached, though later he too was to sire three illegitimate sons.

No thought of emulating the martial careers of his elder brothers entered the mind of Frederick Keppel, the fourth

son of William Anne. While they risked their lives for King
and Country, he remained quietly at home, never deviating
from his maturing ambition to be a bishop. Like Augustus,
he was educated at Westminster School, and matriculated at
Christ Church, Oxford, aged nineteen. In 1752 he took his
B.A. degree, followed by an M.A. two years later; and in
1762 he obtained a D.D. by diploma. Once ordained in the
Church of England, he soon obtained preferment, acting as
chaplain in ordinary to George II (and later to George III).
On 19 April 1754 he was made a canon of Windsor.

Two years later he wrote a letter to the Duke of Newcastle
(First Lord of the Treasury), quietly but firmly refusing to
be moved elsewhere. The Duke had hoped to move him on
to Christ Church but he demurred:

> I flatter myself your Grace would not expect me to do
> anything to my disadvantage, which this certainly
> would be; for by the exchange I should lose fifty pounds
> a year besides the expenses of removing, and the chance
> of Livings falling to our own Gift.
>
> As your Grace was so good as to say I was at liberty
> to do as I thought proper, and at the same time said
> there were many who would be very glad to accept the
> offer: I am in hopes your Grace will not take it amiss if
> I decline leaving Windsor....

And there he stayed for another eight years.

In 1758 he married Laura, the eldest of the three natural
daughters of Horace Walpole's brother, Sir Edward Walpole.
Horace Walpole's favourite was beautiful Maria, first
married to James, 2nd Earl Waldegrave, and then to
George III's brother, the Duke of Gloucester; he damns
Laura with faint praise:

> The bride is very agreeable, and sensible, and good.

Not so handsome as her sisters, but further from ugliness than beauty.

She was to be a thorn in the flesh of her three brothers-in-law.

In August 1761, Sir Edward Walpole wrote to William Pitt to ask if it was 'agreeable to him to make Mr Keppel a bishop at this juncture'. Pitt refused, but four months later Lord Albemarle importuned the Duke of Newcastle, on his brother's behalf '... having heard that the Bishop of St. David's is dead, to have recommended the Poor Old Prebend of Windsor to your Grace's protection. ...' Thomas, Duke of Newcastle was good-natured to the point of weakness. But Frederick Keppel had to wait another year before he was carried to the Bishopric of Exeter on the tide of his brother's victory at Havana.

For neither of William Anne's two surviving daughters did the course of true love run smoothly. Robin Adair (made Surgeon of the Hospital of the Forces in Great Britain in 1756) was already a surgeon of distinction when he met and fell in love with Caroline Keppel. But, in the view of her eldest brother, the nature of his profession and the fact that he had reached the age of forty rendered him ineligible. For Caroline too it had been a case of love at first sight but, as head of the family, Lord Albemarle now decreed that she must give up the idea of marrying Adair, who was forbidden to see her. To get over her infatuation, poor Caroline was sent abroad. Then, when her health deteriorated, she was brought back and sent to Bath, where it was hoped that the waters and the brilliant society she found there would effect her cure. In 1758, when Tenducci, the famous Italian tenor, came to London to sing at Ranelagh Gardens and elsewhere, his rendering of the touching Irish ballad 'Eileen Aroon' became the rage. The song reached Bath and made an immediate impression on Lady Caroline. Adapting her own unhappiness to the melody, she converted the words to suit her case.

> 'What's this dull town to me?
> Robin's not near;
> He whom I wished to see,
> Wished so to hear.
> Where's all the joy and mirth,
> Made life a heaven on earth?
> Oh, they're all fled with thee,
> Robin Adair.'

Two more stanzas were added to her lament, and at last Lord Albemarle relented before such touching fidelity. On 22 February 1759 Lady Caroline Keppel and Robert Adair were married at St. George's, Hanover Square. Three years later, at Ranelagh, Tenducci sang her words set to the original Irish refrain. Adair became a leader of his profession and a friend of George III. In 1760 he was appointed Inspector of the Regimental Infirmaries, and in 1773 Surgeon to the Royal Hospital, Chelsea. But in 1769 he had lost his beloved wife.

In 1764, this time presumably with her eldest brother's blessing, Lady Caroline's younger sister, Elizabeth, married the Marquess of Tavistock. Three years later he died as the result of a hunting accident, and within twelve months his widow died of a broken heart.

4
The Fleet Assembles

There were inevitable but not undue delays in mounting the Havana expedition. Lord Anson had presented his project to the Secret Committee during the first week of January 1762, and directly it was agreed to he ordered the Navy Board to provide 10,000 tons of transport for overseas services at Spithead. By making use of three transports already there and thirty-two ships just arrived from Belleisle, this tonnage was speedily obtained. But the transports from Belleisle had to have ordnance stores unloaded and troops disembarked before they could be ready for further service; and they were all in need of grounding-out and bottom-cleaning before they could be refitted to take troops on board. To add to the delay, there was a general shortage of bedding both at Spithead and Portsmouth, most of it being rotten or eaten by rats. While these difficulties were being surmounted, the Ordnance and Victualling Boards assembled 2,500 tons of ordnance ships, with which to convey engineers, artillerymen and stores; and 'sixteen thousand tons of victuallers were to convey seven months' army rations for sixteen thousand men.' This mammoth undertaking was completed, with the ships loaded and ready to sail from the Thames, after barely three weeks' preparation. But the lack of bedding, now to be supplied from London, held things up and, owing to strong westerly gales, the transports did not reach Spithead until 26 February.

Two days earlier, on 24 February, the Duke of Cumberland

had penned a letter to Lord Albemarle from Windsor Great
Lodge.

My dear Lord,

A thousand thanks for your letter of the 22nd. I have
felt the bad weather that has lasted ever since we parted
—for I have had a sharp attack of the gout; but the
contrary winds were still more unpleasant, as I dread
the loss of one single day at present, and that not the
less for Knowles's company, who is here, and croaking
every day at dinner.

Any bystander would think me the projector and fitter
out of the expedition, but the truth is the subject is so
tender, that I cannot allow even suppositions which are
perhaps not quite groundless. I must not omit saying
that I gave your brother [Augustus] false intelligence
about the Moro Fort, for he asked me whether ships
could anchor before that Port, and I answered in the
negative, but on further enquiry of Knowles, he says
the men of warr may anchor as near as they please in
from four to six fathoms water, though he assured me
he had told your brother, yet I thought it safest to
write you myself.

Dear Albemarle, get away as fast as I wish, judge
whether I don't love my easterly wind more than ever.

Yours, for ever,

WILLIAM

Eventually, when Sir George Pocock's fleet set sail, on
6 March, it seemed surprisingly small in ships and manpower.
There were only five of the line, comprising his flagship
Namur, *Valiant*, *Belleisle*, *Hampton Court* and *Ripon*; and Lord
Albemarle was in command of a mere 4,365 men. On board
was a painter, Dominic Serres, commissioned with the hope
that he would paint the campaign's victories; and John

Kennion, a thirty-year-old merchant of Liverpool and Jamaica who, as 'commissary', had the lucrative contract of 'victualling, arming and clothing the expedition'. (At that time, Liverpool was the leading slave-port of Europe, and already Kennion had shares in ten slave-ships.) The build-up of the fleet was to be effected in transit to Havana. At Martinique ten of the line were to be added under Commodore Swanton, one of Admiral Rodney's commanding officers; and an additional squadron was to be picked up in the Antilles. Lord Albemarle expected to acquire another 8,000 men, seconded, under command of General Monckton, from Sir Jeffrey Amherst's forces in North America to assist Admiral Rodney at Martinique. To these Sir Jeffrey was expected to add another 4,000 troops (though 2,000 of this force, mulattos and slaves, had still to be raised). Off Plymouth, the fleet was joined by the *Burford* and *Florentine*. But when Commodore Keppel made a prize of a French West Indiaman a few days later and sent her into Plymouth under convoy of *Burford*, one of the storeships hit another and had to be taken off, so that the main fleet did not gain in strength by these exchanges.

While Sir George Pocock was assembling his expeditionary force at Spithead, Admiral Rodney was achieving a notable victory at Martinique. He had taken over command from Sir James Douglas, still in command of the Leeward Isles, and, fortified by reinforcements from Belleisle and from Admiral Lord Colville on the American station, he now had under his command eighteen of the line, ten cruisers and four bomb-vessels; while General Monckton commanded about 13,000 troops, not counting 1,000 volunteers and negroes raised by 'the authorities' at Barbados.

Despite the heavily guarded shore of Martinique and the mountainous terrain inside the island, Martinique became a

British possession on 15 February 1762, thanks to the brilliant cooperation of naval and land forces. With the subjection also of Grenada and St. Lucia by two of Admiral Rodney's officers, Commodore Swanton and Captain Augustus Hervey, the power of the French fleet in the West Indies was decisively broken.

In his original orders Admiral Rodney had been told he was to do one of two things in the event of the French fleet's escape from Brest: reinforce Admiral Holmes (Commander-in-Chief Jamaica) or, if the French fleet menaced his own force, call for help from the Jamaica station. On 23 December 1761 the Brest fleet, under Admiral Blénac, had escaped from under the nose of Captain Spry, one of Commodore Keppel's captains; and had headed for the West Indies with all sails set, Keppel's ships being too foul to overtake it. Rodney had been warned of its approach and had prepared to meet it either to the north or the south of Martinique. But Blénac had learnt of the island's defeat and so had approached it on the windward side and had then headed north, full sail, towards Cap François and San Domingo. About 12 March, news reached Rodney from Guadeloupe that Blénac's fleet had been seen steering to westward, which probably meant that he was sailing to Cap François to a 'pre-concerted junction' with Spain and then on to attack Jamaica. Rodney knew that Spain was building up a strong naval contingent at Havana and resolved at all costs to keep the French and Spanish fleets apart. (Thanks to quick action on the part of a British captain who had captured a French privateer on 11 December, Rodney was already in possession of the vital information that Spain had on the previous day ordered the seizure of all British shipping. Captain Johnstone had manned and victualled his prize and had sent her off express to Rodney, thus giving the Admiral advance knowledge of Spain's declaration of war.)

Shortly afterwards an urgent express reached Rodney from the Governor and Council of Jamaica saying that they had learned from intercepted letters that Jamaica was to be attacked by combined French and Spanish forces whose commanding (French) officers were already on board Blénac's fleet. The Jamaican authorities urged Admiral Rodney and General Monckton to help them. In addition, a letter from Captain Forrest, senior officer on the station, informed Rodney that Admiral Holmes had died.

Admiral Rodney's duty seemed clear—to sail to Jamaica's assistance at once with every ship he could spare, and to take with him as many troops as General Monckton would release. Here he came up against the refusal of General Monckton, who felt that he could not 'detach troops from his command without orders from England'. So Rodney went off with ten sail of the line, three frigates and three bomb-vessels, leaving Monckton and his troops with a skeleton force to guard them.

Rodney's intention was to combine with Admiral Holmes's squadron which, with his, would amount to about twenty of the line, equal to the combined squadrons of the enemy. He intended to send Sir James Douglas back to the Caribbean with eight of the line, sufficient to deal with Blénac if he doubled back, or with the other French squadron if it appeared from Rochefort. He sent a message to Captain Forrest (acting commander of the Jamaica squadron) telling him to meet him with all his squadron at Cape Nicholas in the Windward Passage. Then he himself sailed on to St. Kitts, where he intended to divide his force.

He was greeted at St. Kitts by Captain Elphinston of the *Richmond* frigate with new direct orders from home. These told him that a secret expedition was coming out in the middle of April, under the command of Admiral of the Blue Sir George Pocock (late Commander-in-Chief East Indies), with George, Earl of Albemarle, commanding the troops.

Although the orders tempered the news with an apology, they made clear that Admiral Rodney was to be superseded in the supreme command 'as the importance of the enterprise demanded an officer of high rank at its head'. The actual objective was not divulged, and all that Rodney was told was that it was intended to impress the Spanish colonies, and that every other project must be subordinated to it. If Rodney had not yet subdued Martinique, that project too must be suspended.

Rodney himself was to be under Admiral Pocock's orders, and was told to repair at once to Martinique and there to prepare transports for General Monckton's troops. He was also told to organise ten of the line, whose captains were all to be junior to Commodore Swanton, for special services with the enterprise. The orders ended with a strict injunction: 'As you must be sensible of the great importance of these orders it is unnecessary for us to add any motives to enforce the most punctual and expeditious obedience thereto.'

Rodney could not reconcile these orders with the actual situation, which was that the Brest fleet was at Cap François, only waiting to combine with the Spanish forces at Havana to attack a British possession. Moreover, he was convinced that the Government at home did not know this, although it knew that the Brest fleet had escaped the British blockade three months before. With his up-to-date knowledge, it seemed vital to Rodney that immediate help should still be sent to Jamaica. His new orders clearly kept him to his own station, organising a squadron under Swanton to be ready for the arrival of Sir George Pocock. But he decided that Sir James Douglas could still act according to his original orders and hold on for Jamaica. This Sir James did, with ten of the line and with Captain Hervey as his second-in-command.

When Admiral Rodney returned to St. Pierre, Martinique, he found General Monckton mobilising every man who could safely be spared from the island garrisons. He busied himself with the transports, but he was loath to see his squadron lie idle. So, although he had been specifically told to keep Commodore Swanton at the ready at Martinique, 'he despatched him with the greatest part of his remaining ships, to cruise on the Spanish main.' If he intended thereby to increase his prizes, his ambition was still-born.

On 12 April Sir James Douglas reached Port Royal, Jamaica, where he found a squadron of nine sail. There he heard that the Brest fleet was now reduced to six of the line and three frigates, all at Cap François, and that an attack on Jamaica from Havana had been abandoned. He also heard that more troops were expected to come from the North American Station to join the 'grand expedition'. Most importantly, he was able to read for himself the orders from home issued to Holmes, the dead admiral, with the same stringent call to implicit obedience. Holmes had been ordered to raise five hundred negroes to supplement Lord Albemarle's troops; and had been told to await Sir George Pocock's orders, at Port Royal, with his squadron ready to sail.

Like Rodney, with his on-the-spot knowledge, Douglas felt that he should interpret these orders differently, and that his paramount duty was to protect the passage of the North American transports, and to watch out for Blénac. So he too ignored them and despatched Captain Hervey, with seven of the line and ten frigates, to take station at Tortuga, an island lying to leeward of Cap François.

5
Approach to Havana

Despite a violent storm in the Atlantic, Sir George Pocock, with his five ships of the line, thirty transports and as many store-ships, reached Barbados on 20 April still up to time. There he was told of Admiral Rodney's capture of Martinique, and of his decision that Cas Navires Bay, Martinique, should be the rendezvous between his own squadron and that of the Commander-in-Chief. Sir George also found ample stores awaiting him at Barbados, enough to victual his crews for six months. There was a lavish supply of drink for officers and ratings: 600 gallons of rum for the men; and 100 hogshead of claret and 900 casks of wine and some beef for the officers. Having taken all this on board, he sailed at once for Cas Navires Bay and arrived there five days later.

He found all General Monckton's transports ready to sail, with his troops on board. But of Admiral Rodney's fleet and, particularly, of Commodore Swanton's 'ten of the line', there was no sign. Only Rodney's own flagship, *Marlborough*, and three other ships of the line were there, to guard the island; and three 'fifties' badly in need of a refit and due to be sent home with the next convoy. To add to Sir George's exasperation, Rodney sent him word that he was down with fever at St. Pierre, so could not meet him to pay his respects.

The new Commander-in-Chief was faced with a daunting problem. As far as he knew, the Spanish fleet at Havana amounted to twenty of the line, and the Brest fleet was now at Cap François. As a result of Admiral Rodney's high-handed action, Pocock would have to conduct a combined operation against two fleets, with his own fleet not up to the strength of either of them. With Rodney's units so widely dispersed that it was impossible for him to recall them to Martinique, Admiral Pocock knew that he was also responsible for the safe conduct of the Jamaica convoy, and for that of about fifty commercial vessels waiting at St. Kitts. Rodney had completely upset Lord Anson's meticulously prepared plan, which was based on an initial naval concentration outside the danger zone.

In viewing the Havana campaign as a whole, Lord Anson had concentrated on three main points. First, its navigational and seasonal difficulties dependent on the trade winds and the tropical hazards of wind and weather; secondly, the tactical advantage of approach; and thirdly, how to instil maximum confusion in the enemy.

The ordinary route from the Windward Islands to Havana lay to leeward, past Jamaica and through the Yucatan Channel with 'an easy beat back of some two hundred and fifty miles with the current along the north-western end of Cuba'. This was the route pursued by homing British convoys. So if a British attack on Cuba were to be considered, in the ordinary way the enemy would expect it to start with a concentration at Port Royal, Jamaica, but with a squadron kept off Cap François to blockade Admiral Blénac and to cover the passage from North America for Sir Jeffery Amherst's troops. Should the enemy see no concentration at Jamaica, he would think he had no immediate cause for alarm. Lord Anson was fully aware of the difficulty of a concentration of allied fleets, and for the French and Spanish admirals this was apparent from the start. Each admiral counted upon a concentration, but at a point best suited to his own interests. Blénac had left France before war with Spain had been declared, and he had come out primarily to save what he could of French island territory. The Spanish Captain-

General, Don Juan de Prado Porto Correro, was charged
with the defence of Havana. He had twelve of the line (not
twenty, as had been reported to Admiral Pocock) and eight
sail. At Santiago, at the opposite end of the island of Cuba,
he had three of the line; and there were one or two big ships
at Vera Cruz, Mexico. But all these were under the overall
command of Don Gutierre de Hevia, Marques del Real
Transporte, who, with de Prado, had come out as Commander-in-Chief of the American squadrons. His orders were
to keep the Havana squadron at the ready but not to risk unnecessary sorties. Both he and de Prado had received their instructions six months before. On the declaration of war with
Britain later orders had been sent out to them, but Captain
Johnstone's astute warning had alerted Admiral Rodney to
intercept them. The *Milford* had engaged the *Aviso*, carrying
the new orders, off San Domingo and forced her to strike.
Her commander sank his despatches, and the Spanish admirals were left in ignorance until a copy of the Madrid
Gazette reached them, containing the declaration of war.

As Admiral Rodney and Sir James Douglas were fully
aware, the prevailing wind was a favourable factor in keeping the allies apart. Though it would be easy for Blénac to
run down to Havana, it would be very difficult for the
Spanish Admiral de Hevia to beat up to Cap François and,
with Captain Hervey's squadron blockading the French admiral in port, Blénac's appeals to de Hevia to extricate him
fell on deaf ears. Neither de Hevia nor de Prado would move
from their established positions. Unless they got news of a
British concentration at Port Royal, Jamaica, nothing was
going to bring them out. But Lord Anson, in his master plan
for the attack on Havana, had instructed Admiral Pocock
to approach from a totally unexpected direction: from the
north.

Anson intended the Admiral's concentration with Sir

James Douglas to be at Cape St. Nicholas in the Windward Passage, between San Domingo and Cuba, and for the fleet then to approach Havana from the northern, windward, side. He based his daring plan on an old Spanish chart in his possession, probably acquired through the capture of one of his early prizes. This lay through a treacherous narrow passage called the Old Bahama Channel, where it was known that already many a rich ship had foundered. The Spaniards considered the route too dangerous for any large ship to sail through, but for those brave enough to risk the hazards it had certain distinct advantages: no beat back; before the wind the whole way; and a much shorter distance to cover, so gaining vital time before the hurricanes set in. For the British admiral, an attack from the Old Bahama Channel on Havana would carry the supreme advantage of surprise.

Meanwhile, preparations at Martinique proceeded in an atmosphere of tension.

On arrival, Lord Albemarle found the condition of the troops very unsatisfactory. There was a high degree of sickness mainly caused by the consumption of bad rum. Many of the regiments were incomplete, lacking in 'all sorts of camp equipment' and generally complaining of the poor quality of their arms. Moreover, they had been paid only up to 24 February, so that Lord Albemarle had to advance General Monckton £10,000. As he wrote to Sir Jeffery Amherst he himself had money to pay his own troops to 24 May, but thereafter he would be dependent on Sir Jeffery's Paymaster-General, North America, for further funds.

Meanwhile he objected to General Monckton's arrangements and spent the next fortnight reorganising his transport dispositions, fitting out horse transports, and getting more troops from Dominica. And, as General Monckton's health had deteriorated, he gave him leave to return to New York, and put Brigadier Rufane in command of the remaining forces at Martinique.

Admiral Pocock got his own back on Admiral Rodney by comandeering his flagship, *Marlborough*, and then (much to Rodney's disgust) squeezing him and his staff into a 'sixty-four'. Thus, with two ships of the line awaiting him at St. Kitts, Sir George brought up his battle strength to eight ships of the line. He hoped that this would be superior in strength to Blénac's squadron. He issued an order whereby the ships in the West Indies and North American squadrons could distinguish each other:

> The ship to windward to hoist a Dutch flag at the main-top-masthead.
> The ship to leeward to answer by hoisting an English ensign at the fore-top-masthead.

On 6 May, sending forward orders for the convoy to meet him at Basse Terre Road, St. Kitts, Sir George Pocock sailed on his hazardous expedition. Two days later he arrived at St. Kitts, according to plan. There he found awaiting him the two ships of the line and the Jamaica convoy which, all told, put him in charge of some two hundred sail. Lord Albemarle, in charge of the land forces, found himself responsible for five brigades of infantry, numbering nearly 12,000 men, besides engineers, artillery and military stores. Nor was this all, as he expected over 2,000 more to be sent to him from North America and Jamaica.

With what has been described as 'this unwieldy armada', Sir George Pocock wasted no time. Keeping to windward of San Domingo, he sailed through the Mona Passage and made Cape St. Nicholas on 17 May. Here a letter awaited him from Sir James Douglas, acknowledging his orders and informing the Admiral that he was about to join him with nine of the line. Moreover, Sir James had given the rendezvous to

Captain Hervey who, with his seven of the line, was still blockading Cap François. Being dissatisfied with the quality of the pilots he had obtained to take the fleet through the Old Bahama Channel, Sir James on his own initiative had despatched Captain Elphinston in the *Richmond* frigate 'to survey it as far to leeward as Cay Sal', where the five hundred miles of dangerous navigation came to an end.

On 18 May Captain Hervey joined the secret expedition, reporting that Admiral Blénac was still in Cap François. As Sir James Douglas had leave to go home, Sir George Pocock decided to put him in command of the homeward-bound Jamaica convoy, intending to send him back by the orthodox route, through the Yucatan and Florida Channels.

All this, of course, depended on Admiral Blénac remaining idle in Cap François. But Sir James Douglas had been credibly informed that the French admiral was so incensed at finding that his Spanish ally, de Hevia, had gone to Havana instead of joining him, that he had announced that, were he not soon to unite his forces with those of Spain, he would return home with the French trade vessels.

On 26 May news reached Sir George Pocock that Sir Jeffery Amherst and his troops were about to sail from North America but, in his secret orders, Sir George had been instructed not to wait for the American transports. Thanks to Admiral Rodney's action in sending Commodore Swanton to sail the Spanish Main, Sir George's strength was too weak to release ships to protect Amherst's transports. So on 27 May he sailed north with his whole fleet through the Windward Passage, after detaching Sir James Douglas and the homegoing convoy to Port Royal, Jamaica.

Captain Elphinston met Sir George Pocock's fleet the day after it sailed. He had been right up the Old Bahama Channel to Cay Sal and back, and now produced a complete survey of the Channel, with sketches of land and cays on both sides of it. By so doing, he now had positive proof that Lord Anson's chart was correct.

Following the method used by Vice-Admiral Sir Charles Saunders on the St. Lawrence river, Sir George Pocock now organised his transports into seven divisions, each with its conducting men-of-war. There was no regular vanguard or rearguard in their formation, the plan being to concentrate nine of the line in the van or centre. In the first division were four of the line under Pocock (*Namur*), plus transports of light infantry, three battalions of grenadiers, two hospital ships and three artillery ships. Only Commodore Keppel's ship of the line (*Valiant*) led the second division, conducting the 1st Brigade, two hospital ships, three artillery ships and four sail. Captain Joseph Knight (*Belleisle*), leading the third division, was allocated three of the line, conducting the 2nd Brigade, one hospital ship and three artillery ships. Captain Barton (*Téméraire*), in the fourth division, was allocated one ship of the line and a large consignment of storeships, negro transports, horse transports, baggage transports and four ships with fascines. Captain Barker (*Culloden*), in the fifth division, was similarly allocated one ship of the line to conduct the 3rd Brigade, one hospital ship and two transports of artillery. But between them the sixth division (Captain Goostrey, *Cambridge*) and the seventh division (Captain Burnet, *Marlborough*) had eight of the line and two 'fifties' to strengthen their coverage of the 4th and 5th Brigades, two hospital ships and five ships with artillery. The reason for this double strengthening was to guard against a possible attack from windward from the rear by Admiral Blénac.

Blénac remained sulking inside Cap François and Pocock's fleet proceeded without hindrance, thanks to Captain Elphinston. His foresight had been remarkable, even making possible the passage of the narrowest and most dangerous part of the Channel (between Cay Lobos and Cay Comfite) by night, by means of lighter beacons burning upon the rocks. By the evening of 5th June, a week after leaving Cape Nicholas, the whole fleet was clear of Cay Sal and in sight of Matanzas, less than 100 miles from Havana.

The same day, in accordance with their Sovereign's decree, Admiral of the Blue Sir George Pocock and Lieutenant-General Lord Albemarle drew up and signed on board the *Namur* a formal document which, should the Havana enterprise prove successful, aimed at an equal distribution of 'plunder and booty' between sea and land forces under their command. To the commanders-in-chief, five-fifteenth parts of the whole were to be equally divided, to include distributions to the wounded officers and men in both services, and pensions to widows. To Commodore the Hon. Augustus Keppel and to Lieutenant-General George Eliott, seconds-in-command, sea and land, one-fifteenth part each was to be allocated. The remainder to be distributed equally between captains, officers, seamen and marines; and officers and soldiers of the land forces concerned.

It was on the very next day, 6 June, that Viscount Anson, whose genius had inspired the whole expedition, died in England of a lingering illness.

6

The Landing

Lord Albemarle had as his chief engineer Lieutenant-Colonel Patrick Mackellar who had served in the same capacity at Quebec and Martinique. On his own assertion, serving under Mackellar as his assistant was Thomas Mante. In a subsequent campaign, again on his own assertion, Mante rose to the rank of major and wrote his *History of the Late War in North America*. But it is as the eyewitness historian of the Havana expedition that we are indebted to him.

He describes the sailing of Sir George Pocock's fleet from Spithead on 6 March, the violent storm it ran into in the Atlantic, and its arrival at Barbados and then Martinique; and he lists ships and commanding officers, regiments and numbers incorporated in Sir George Pocock's command, as it weathered the perils of the Old Bahama Channel.

All went well. On 2 June, the *Alarm* and *Echo*, sailing ahead to lie on the Cay Sal bank, spotted 'five sail in the N.W. quarter'. *Alarm* (under the command of Captain Alms) made a signal. Then both he and Captain Lendrick (*Echo*) gave chase. *Alarm* engaged the Spanish frigate *Thetis* (of twenty-two guns and 200 men) and the *Phoenix* (a storeship armed for war, of eighteen guns and seventy-five men) and within the hour both ships struck to her. There were casualties on both sides, but valuable information was gained from the captured crews. From them Admiral Pocock learned that the Spaniards had sixteen men-of-war in the harbour at Havana 'almost ready for sea; that they were not in the least in expectation of a visit from the English and that the garrison

consisted of very few troops. . . .' Two other vessels were also
captured and another one escaped. Mante declares that by it
the Governor of Havana would have been 'certainly informed' of the advent of the British Navy. With the value of
hindsight, subsequent historians are agreed that this information arrived too late to be of use to the Spaniards, who were
taken completely by surprise on 6 June.

Always mindful of the health and welfare of his crews, Commodore Keppel while in transit sent out vigorous signals to
improve their condition. Beginning on 20 May, he lists seventeen ships to which provisions are to be delivered, with drastic
orders to scrap inferior food.

He orders the masters of *Alarm* and two other ships 'to survey beef pork and butter' on board the frigate *Dover* and 'if
found to be as represented to throw beef and pork into the
sea and deliver the butter to the boatswain for the ship's use'.

He orders the masters of *Téméraire*, *Ripon* (always spelt by
him with two 'p's) and *Thunder* 'to survey beer on board the
Constant Jane transport and if found as represented to stack
it into the sea'.

The master of *Dragon* is to survey 'bread flour and oatmeal
on board the *Prince Edward* hospital ship' and 'if as represented to be left with the Master for Sir George Pocock to
dispose [of]'.

He orders a survey of the bread on board the '*Prince of
Brunswick* victualler'. Thereafter a report is to be made to him
in writing whether the damage is due to its being improperly
stowed, or to any defect in the ship.

Following a letter from Captain Randall, Agent for Transports, telling him that 'the greater part of the Masters of the
Transports . . . from Martinique have reported that their provisions on board are so bad that the troops have refused to
eat them', Keppel orders the masters of *Dragon*, *Ripon* and

Trent to go on board these ships, to report back to him as to what is and is not fit for use.

These and similar orders continue in meticulous detail right through from start to finish of the Havana campaign.

To quote Mante, Havana was situated 'exactly under the Tropic of Cancer, 83° west of London'. He goes on to say that the town was 'by far the most considerable place in the West Indies, with docks in which ships of war of the first magnitude are built' and a harbour 'spacious enough to receive an 100 ships of the line'. He reiterates what was already universally known, that the town was 'the key to the riches of Mexico... till their final embarkation to Spain'.

The harbour lay to the east of the town, with its entrance defended by the formidable fortress of El Morro (constructed in the 1590s, as a defence against Sir Francis Drake). This was built to the north on a sheer point of rock, inaccessible from the sea, and was large enough to garrison 1,000 men. Engineer Mante comments further that it contained 'very good casements and two cisterns which afford plenty of water. It is fortified to the east with two bastions, a courtin, and good covered way, with a dry ditch, half of which is cut out of the solid rock.' Subsequently, his measurements of the width and depth of the ditch make sober reading:

Facing the sea:	depth	$63\frac{1}{2}$ ft.
	breadth at bottom	43 ft.
	breadth at top	56 ft.
Facing the centre curtain:	depth	$56\frac{1}{2}$ ft.
	breadth at bottom	43 ft.
	breadth at top	105 ft.
Facing the land bastion:	depth	45 ft.
	breadth at bottom	35 ft.
	breadth at top	$43\frac{1}{2}$ ft.

How these obstacles were overcome was a triumph of naval
and military ingenuity, and of heroic endurance by British
soldiers and seamen.

Thomas Mante continues his survey:

> ... on the Moro side is a battery built of stone called the
> Twelve Apostles; and a little higher up, another called
> the Shepherd's Battery; above these a chain of hills
> called the Cavannos extend themselves from the Moro
> to the plains of Guanabacoa. These hills command
> the town and docks, and can always be protected by
> the ships in port ... anchorage for men of war of the
> first rate and being without defended by a steep hill
> called Gonzales.

To the east of El Morro, the coast was well wooded, but
interspersed with small villages set amid cultivated fields.
These were dominated by 'a prodigious number of country
houses'.

Across the harbour, to the west, a chain of bastions and
other fortifications defended the city. Most of the surrounding earth had been removed to build its ramparts, thus only
leaving patches of marshy ground and barren rock. Facing El
Morro was the fort of La Punta, with a battery of guns guarding the boom; and a few hundred yards along the water-
front was the North Gate bastion, guarding the Governor's
castle.

As the British fleet approached Havana, the Governor of
Cuba and his officials were attending Mass in the parish
church. When they were told that a large number of ships
had appeared on the horizon to the north of the Castle of El
Morro, they assumed that it was a friendly convoy 'merely
in passage'. But when further information reached them that
the friendly convoy had flat boats filled with troops in tow,

they were seized with panic, mobilising the garrison, calling out the militia and searching for mounts for the dragoons.

Over a year had passed since the Governor, Don Juan de Prado, and the admiral, Don Gutierre de Hevia, had come out, accompanied by two French engineers, with elaborate instructions to repair and improve the defences of Havana. But little had been achieved. The weakest point in the Havana defences was the rocky ridge of the Cabaña Hill (Mante's 'Cavannos'), running along the east side of the harbour opposite the city. This was high enough to command nearly all the defences of the city and harbour, but it was not yet fortified. The official scheme of defence provided a strong redoubt at its inner and landward end, with El Morro dominating its other extremity. But until the *Gazette* arrived from Spain with news of the declaration of war on England, the scheme had not got beyond discussion. An effort had then been made to clear the site for the redoubt, but this was shortlived owing to an outbreak of yellow fever among some labourers and troops drafted in from Mexico.

Both de Prado and de Hevia had orders primarily to protect Havana, so their contacts with their French ally, Admiral Blénac, at Cap François had been only cursory. Secure, as they thought, from any sudden assault from the west, neither they nor their staffs had considered the possibility of a large fleet able to navigate the Old Bahama Channel to the north. When it did so, their consternation was complete.

On the evening of 6 June, Don Juan held a hurried council of war. Present were the retiring Viceroy of Peru, the Conde de Superunda; the retiring Governor of Cartagena (Colombia), Diego de Tabarres; and the admiral in command, Don Gutierre de Hevia. In the harbour lay 100 richly-laden merchant vessels. To protect these, the Council decided to block the harbour's entrance by sinking three large ships across its mouth. By so doing, the entire Spanish fleet was immobilised inside the harbour, a godsend to an invading force. Then, in mild mitigation of this lunatic act, the Council decided to use the sailors and guns on board the sunken vessels to reinforce the land defences.

Yellow fever had reduced the number of the garrison to 3,000 regular soldiers; to these 9,000 sailors were now added, but only about 3,000 militia. Only 2,000 muskets were available for the whole force, so pikes and machetes had to be issued to supplement its weapons of defence. Many of the militiamen were negroes or mulattos, and de Prado enrolled and armed a number of slaves as well, promising them their liberty if they would fight. As the Cabaña Hill was unfortified, he decided to defend it with cannon, detailing 1,000 sailors from the fleet to drag up guns. But, in the general confusion, no one thought out ways of protecting the working parties against enemy attack.

The concept of the capture of Havana had been inspired by Admiral Sir Charles Knowles (to whose 'croaking' at dinner the Duke of Cumberland had referred in his letter of 24 February to Lord Albemarle). Later he was to criticise violently Lord Albemarle's direction of the campaign. But in his initial report Sir Charles himself was guilty of two glaring omissions: he made no mention either of the gigantic size of the ditch defending the seaboard side of El Morro, or of the total absence of fresh water to slake the thirst of troops and crews in the tropical heat.

Colonel Mackellar was detailed to evolve a plan of attack for the British and, after a general survey based on the nearest places where ships could anchor, his memorandum gave two possible landing-places: to the east of Havana, at the mouth of the Coximar river; or to the west of the city at Chorera (though this was said to be built on foul ground). He eliminated as impossible the project of investing the city and El

Morro together, for this operation would need a much bigger force to carry it through. But, as he felt that any attack on the city would fail unless El Morro had been captured, he advocated that an attack on that fortress should be made first. There were formidable initial difficulties before this objective could be achieved. The barren rock, on which the fortress was built without soil, would make siege tactics doubly difficult. Mackellar added urgent memoranda to find out whether there was any fresh water 'to be got in or near Coximar Bay', or whether there were any springs, wells, rivers or ponds, 'and at what distance'. To the south of El Morro there was the unfortified ridge of the Cabaña Hill dominating the town and harbour; from this (if guns could be mounted along it) the land-side of El Morro could be bombarded, and the city and part of the harbour as well. If this line of attack were adopted, Mackellar felt that the main landing for assault troops would have to be at Coximar, where the fleet could anchor in some shelter. This was also the nearest possible point from which to get supplies. Fort Chorera, west of the city, was four miles further away from El Morro, and there the fleet would have to anchor along shore without shelter. Even so, Mackellar realised that this fort too would have to be captured, as it commanded the main water-supply to the town.

According to Mante, the *Valiant* was the first vessel to spot the land at Coximar and Commodore Keppel went on board the flagship, *Namur*, to announce the discovery to the Admiral, 'in a transport of joy', and with eyes which 'flashed fire as he spoke'. He then returned to his own ship and made a signal to all his captains, and also to his brother, the General, to come on board, at the same time ordering his ship's crew to be called aft. Then, 'waving his hat above his head', he so addressed them: 'Courage, my lads! The day is ours. The

Admiral has given us leave to take yonder town, with all the treasure in it; so we have nothing to do now, but make our fortune as fast as we can, for the place can never hold out against us. The purser will give every brave fellow a can of punch, to drink prosperity to Old England.... We shall all be as rich as Jews. The place is paved with gold....' Whereupon the crew answered, with three cheers and went 'skipping and dancing for joy' to get their punch. To the look-out man who had first spotted the land, the Commodore gave a golden guinea. As his ordinary rate of pay was fifteen pence a day, this man achieved an instant bonus of seventeen days' pay.

Mante stresses the point that 'there not being on board the whole [British] fleet a single man acquainted with the coast [of Cuba], nor any spot being as yet absolutely fixed on for the making of a descent, the *Alarm* and *Richmond* were sent with Colonels Carleton and Howe to reconnoitre the shore.'

On 6 June Mackellar's journal reads that '... the fleet arrived within sight of two small forts to the eastward of the Havana situated upon two rivers about 3 miles distant from each other.' (These were the rivers, with the defending forts, of Bacuranoa and Coximar.) It goes on to say that 'the whole fleet was brought to', and that then Admiral Sir George Pocock 'with 12 sail of the line, some frigates, and all the store-ships' bore away to make a feint at the mouth of the Chorera river, west of the town of Havana. 'With 7 sail of the line and several small frigates' Commodore Keppel was ordered to remain with the transports 'and conduct the debarkation of the troops'. But as there was too much wind and too great a swell of surf to effect a landing that night, the Commodore deferred it to 'the point of day'.

The same evening he sent a signal to Captain Goodall in the frigate *Mercury* to proceed immediately inshore and in the morning, when he first perceived the flat boats carrying the troops inland, to bombard 'a battery about four miles to the eastward of the battery of Coximar [Fort Bacuranoa]' and 'endeavour to silence and continue before it that it may in no way annoy His Majesty's troops while they are landing'. The Commodore then shifted his pennant to the *Richmond*, to be nearer the operational scene.

At 6 a.m. on 7 June the first wave of troops 'totalling 3,963 infantry, light infantry, grenadiers, and attached units of engineers and artillery' embarked in flat-bottomed boats. Covered by the *Valiant, Dragon, Téméraire, Orford, Pembroke, Ripon, Dover, Richmond, Trent, Mercury, Bonetta*, and three bomb-vessels, at 9 a.m. the assault craft began to move towards the shore, to a point between the Bacuranoa and Coximar rivers. The *Bonetta* and the bomb-vessel *Basilisk* now joined the *Mercury* in bombarding Fort Bacuranoa, while the *Richmond* and *Trent* started firing at the intended landing-place and the woods behind it. The centre of operations in the fleet was directed by Captain Hervey (*Dragon*); the right wing by Captain Barton (*Téméraire*); the left wing by Captain Arbuthnot (*Orford*) and Captain Jekyll (*Ripon*); and the reserve and rear by Captain Wheelock (*Pembroke*). Under the command of Major-General the Hon. William Keppel and Lieutenant-General George Eliott, the first wave of troops landed at 10 a.m., while their Commander-in-Chief, Lord Albemarle, watched their progress from the barge of the Commodore's ship, *Valiant*.

The first wave of troops met very little opposition, and by three o'clock that afternoon most of the remaining infantry had been landed, without the loss of a single man. They started to advance along the beach but were checked at Coximar. The mouth of the Coximar river was defended by an old stone fort, manned by 600 men with several pieces of cannon. The usual manoeuvre would have been to attack the Spaniards with British infantry and artillery, but Lord Albemarle decided to 'blast them out with naval gun-fire'.

In his brief report of 7 June to Sir George Pocock, Lord Albemarle asked for more artillery and for ordnance ships. Later that evening Commodore Keppel reported to the Admiral in more detail.

> Sir, the fort of Coximar having proved an impediment to Lord Albemarle's crossing the river with the army, determined me to order the *Dragon* with two of the bomb vessels, the *Mercury*, and the *Bonetta* to attack it, and I have now the pleasure to acquaint you that the army are passing the river and taking post on the Morro side. In this last service as well as in the first, I must in justice to Capt. Hervey say that he has acted with judgment and spirit; after having very well cannonaded the Coximar I allowed him to land with his marines, when he took posession of the fort and ground around it, by which the army was allowed to pass the river unmolested. I believe Lord Albemarle will scarce advance tonight as the troops are a little fatigued and it is growing dark. . . .'

Already on 2 June Dominic Serres had sketched out Sir George Pocock's fleet, in its entirety, as it passed through the Old Bahama Channel. Now on 7 June he began the first of his 'victory' series, the landing on Coximar beach. A talented young artist, Lieutenant Philip Orsbridge of H.M.S. *Orford*, executed his prints.

7
Manoeuvres before a Siege

In Sir Charles Knowles's original report to Lord Anson, he had recommended the landing at Coximar: '. . . a small sandy bay called Cojimar, in which is tolerable good anchoring with the common sea breezes. In the middle of the bay is a fort or redoubt with about 8 or 10 guns, with stone very high and of good masonry with a ditch round it; and on the east point is another smaller redoubt with about 5 or 6 guns [Bacuranoa] which I believe is not within gunshot of the other.' He goes on to say: 'Close to Cojimar redoubt is a small river near which is the most convenient place for landing a body of troops, all along the coast there being no anchoring with a fleet of transport to anywhere else. This fort I apprehend may be quickly silenced and taken by 2 or 3 '60 or 70' gunships, after which the troops can be landed under the protection of our own canon [*sic*].'

From there he charted a westward course: '. . . a road or path which leads directly to the Moro Castle, the ground rising gradually all the way some distance from the waterside.' He described it as 'a little woody though not very high or seemingly thick'. Then he comes to the crux of his inquiries.

To the left, through the skirt of this wood, I have been informed there is another path which leads to the top of the Stone Quarry hills called Los Cavernos, that lay opposite the City. These hills domineer [*sic*] over the Moro, as well as the city, and indeed command the whole harbour. It will therefore be highly proper to seize upon this situation as speedily as possible after the troops are landed as there is no other ground from where the place can be attacked with like advantage and, in marching up to it, I don't apprehend the troops can be annoyed from the Moro, if they can be seen at all. Between the hill which that fortress stands upon and the Stone Quarry hills, there is a flat of about 300 yards in form of an amphitheatre, from whence the stone from the quarry is put into boats or upon rafts and carried [a]cross the harbour for the use of the city and buildings and fortifications, so that a battery raised upon those hills will not be more than 400 yards from the Moro, if as much, and will batter it on the weakest side.

Two batteries, according to Sir Charles, were mounted on the afore-mentioned 'flat', 'constructed for raking of ships who shall attempt to force into the harbour; one, the Apostles' Battery, of 12 guns; the other, the Shepherd's Battery, of 14 guns, both large metal.' He considered it essential that these should be overcome immediately. Thereafter he was confident that the 'space of ground' on which they stood would be sufficient whereon to mount several batteries to attack El Morro and the town; and wide enough to encamp 'the major part of the troops requisite for the attack, who cannot be hurt by shot either with shells, or annoyed'.

His thesis seems simple. And in a country riddled with malaria and where the hurricane season was fast approaching, the time factor in it was all-important. As he says later: 'Experience in former expeditions might have taught them [the British land forces] that whatever is to be effected in the West Indies must be done as expeditiously as possible.'

But Lord Albemarle, Commander-in-Chief of the land forces at Havana, had a one-track mind.

From the moment of the arrival of Admiral Pocock's fleet at Coximar Bay, the weather had been against it, with thunder and lightning playing on the landing force, and winds and currents straggling the transports. As many of Lord Albemarle's troops were already sick with dysentery and malaria, contracted at Martinique, it did not help their condition to have to lie on their arms in pouring rain on their first night on land.

Once the Coximar fort had been overcome, Sir Charles Knowles had recommended an immediate advance on 'the Stone Quarry hills' dominating the fortress of El Morro; and with this Colonel Mackellar's memorandum had agreed. But, according to Mackellar's journal of 8 June, Lord Albemarle deviated from this project, and early that morning marched the main body of his army about six miles south to the village of Guanabacoa. He detached Colonel Carleton with a small contingent of infantrymen and grenadiers to cut through the Coximar wood and to attack a large body of enemy troops said to be assembled between the British army and the village. Spanish records belittle Mackellar's estimate that Spanish forces numbered about 6,000 men 'chiefly militia mounted, with the Regiment of Edinburgh Dragoons, two companies of grenadiers, and many Spanish officers. . . .' But they could not deny that Colonel Carleton and his light infantry routed their forces and took the village. Lord Albemarle then detailed Lieutenant-General Eliott to remain there, in command of a corps.

The object of Lord Albemarle's manoeuvre had been to secure the southern flank of his army while it besieged El Morro and (to quote Mackellar) 'to secure the avenues on that side, and a large tract of country which could supply the army with water, cattle and vegetables.' Mante adds a note: 'His Lordship then having brought with him from England a number of saddles and bridles, formed a troop of light horse, consisting of 100. The horses were taken from the Spaniards and proved of great service. . . .' Lord Albemarle's first manoeuvre is sharply criticised by Sir Charles Knowles who condemned the relegation of General Eliott and his corps to Guanabacoa as 'permanently dividing the army', while his segregation precluded his whole corps from taking part in the subsequent siege.

On 9 June Lord Albemarle marched the main body of his troops back from Guanabacoa to the woods between Coximar and El Morro. From there Colonel the Hon. William Howe reconnoitred the ground in front of the fortress.

On the preceding night (8 June) British forces had probed the foot of La Cabaña ridge, causing panic among the Spanish seamen sent up to man the guns. They fired wildly 'at noises in the night', causing the Spanish warships in the harbour to bombard the battery, thinking it was under enemy attack. Then, at 1 a.m. on 9 June, the sailors spiked their guns, threw them into the harbour and decamped, leaving the battery undefended.

In his diversionary capacity, Admiral Pocock had been active too. As we have seen, he had sailed on 7 June towards Chorera, 'with twelve ships of the line, several frigates, ordnance ships, victuallers, and storeships'. Since then (as he wrote to Lord Albemarle on 9 June) he had kept the enemy 'upon the alarm' as much as possible by lowering boats filled with marines and rowing them towards the shore; and by sending frigates close in-shore with boats sounding, to delude the Spaniards into thinking that an attack was imminent on the town from the west side. From his point of vantage he had watched 'a body' march out of the fortress the previous night, to set fire to 'every hut and brush wood upon the hill'. He had seen a small magazine blown up, and observed that 'all are marched away'. He yearned for the chance to land '3 or 4000 men on this side of the town', but he knew that this was impossible until 'our American troops' turned up. (Of Sir Jeffery Amherst's reinforcements there was still no sign.)

On the evening of 10 June he began a large-scale diversion. To the west of Havana, warships attacked the forts of Chorera and San Lazaro; grape-shot swept the woods behind possible landing-places; and bomb-vessels threw shells into the northern section of the town. As day broke, marines embarked as though for a large-scale landing, and by noon a small party of them had landed and had briefly occupied the fort at Chorera. All this was to divert attention from Colonel Carleton's intended assault on La Cabaña hill the same night.

Earlier that day Lord Albemarle had sent Sir George Pocock a message telling him that should he, as he hoped, get possession of La Cabaña hill, he would then send about 1,500 men 'round to land in the west with your marines', when he considered that 'Colonel Howe will do very well with such a chosen corps'. The Admiral had promptly approved Lord Albemarle's plan, declaring that in his opinion 'no person can be chose [*sic*] more proper to command... than Colonel Howe'.

On 11 June, headed '$\frac{1}{2}$ past three', Lord Albemarle addressed Admiral Pocock from his headquarters at Coximar:

Dear Sir,

The pass to La Cabaña hill was taken about an hour ago with very little loss. I believe you have alarmed them on the other side very much; the works of the town were manned all night. I shall send Colonel Howe to-morrow to reconnoiter on your side.

In what appears to be Commodore Keppel's journal of the same date, Colonel Carleton's valiant action is described:

Colonel Carleton attacked and took possession of the heights of La Cabaña, where the enemy had cleared away some ground, intending a redoubt. As these heights partly commanded El Morro, but entirely the town and harbour, this attack was conducted with that skill and bravery which Colonel Carleton has manifested on many occasions, and the loss he had in the attack is scarce to be mentioned.

In recognition of his brilliant action, Colonel Carleton was promoted to brigadier.

As Sir Charles Knowles had predicted, by the capture of La Cabaña the British had obtained a major tactical advantage. Now their guns could bombard the eastern part of the harbour, the southern and weakest side of the fortress of El Morro, and the city of Havana itself.

No body of people was more conscious of this than the Spaniards themselves and the Captain-General at Havana almost gave up hope. But, having sealed the ineffectiveness of his fleet by isolating it inside the harbour, de Hevia at long last bestirred himself to take over the defence of Havana, supplanting the nervous officers of the garrison with captains from his ships. One of them, Don Luis Vicente de Velasco, 'a vetern captain of the old war', he put in command of the fortress of El Morro. Then, with England's amphibious triumphs at Quebec, Belleilse and Martinique fresh in their minds, the Spaniards waited fearfully for another brilliantly conceived *coup de main* to be mounted between Admiral Pocock's and Lord Albemarle's sea and land forces. But none came.

Lord Albemarle's experience of warfare had been confined to the Duke of Cumberland's rigid tactics in the Low Countries, and the lightning cut and thrust of simultaneous operations on land and sea was unknown to him. The need in a tropical climate to achieve quick results by such operations was equally outside his experience. Technically, he was correct in deciding to reduce El Morro by siege before he attacked Havana, but to attack a fortress of such strength would inevitably prolong his campaign and tropical diseases were already taking toll of his men. At the outset, he could quote Sir Charles Knowles's opinion that a landing on the western side of the harbour would be impossible, owing to the foul ground off the shore. But on 11 June Sir George Pocock's marines landed there without ill effects, and seized the village at the mouth of the Chorera river to use as their watering-place; and thereafter they found good anchorage all along the coast. They also found that on the western side of the city many of the walls, originally designed to resist buccaneers, were low and old and crumbling. With the heights of La Cabaña about to fall into British hands, there were members in both services (and indeed some of the Spaniards themselves) who felt that a quick kill directed from east and west was feasible. Lord Albemarle could not contemplate such innovations of attack. For him there was a prior objective: the reduction of El Morro, before all else.

Commodore Keppel now directed his squadron to start landing artillery stores and equipment requisite for the siege; and working parties of soldiers and seamen began building roads on which to transport guns, ammunition and stores from the beach to La Cabaña. At this point, as originally decreed by Lord Ligonier, Major-General the Hon. William Keppel took command of the operations against El Morro. On 12 June, to cover the eastern end of Havana and in order to protect the British attack on El Morro from bombardment by Spanish warships, batteries began to be constructed on the Cabaña ridge, known to the British since early that day as 'the Spanish Redoubt'. Under cover of the woods about 250 yards from the fortress, further attempts were made to erect batteries. The density of the woods and the lack of earth with which to fill sandbags greatly hampered this work. And a note of exasperation shows in Commodore Keppel's journal of that date:

> Two howitzers were getting on La Cabaña to prevent the enemy's shipping from placing themselves to annoy our working parties. Some stragglers of the enemy's dragoons and mounted peasantry lurked about the woods and took several seamen belonging to our transports, who were plundering and marauding and which no orders or threats could prevent. Heavy cannon were landing to-day, and heavy work it was to get them over the rocky shore.

This difficulty is emphasised by Thomas Mante: '... Parties were ordered to cut fascines and collect earth... a great labour, the country hereabouts being little better than bare rock and the soil, where any was to be found, exceedingly thin.'

On 9 June Captain Hervey in the *Dragon* had reported to Commodore Keppel that 'in running down within a mile of the shore towards El Morro Castle' he could get no soundings, and that when he had tried to get near 'that angle of the fort that faces the N.' the garrison's fire had obliged him to haul off. But it had seemed to him that, if ships could have soundings to anchor, there was 'very little fire to prevent three ships from placing themselves on such a line with the N. angle as may enable them afterwards to render useless the face of the redan.' He further reported that the redan had eight pieces of cannon in addition to the curtain, which had eleven, but that apart from this artillery he could see nothing 'of... importance against our ships'. Indeed he was of opinion that the three ships might lead 'to an escalade on that side, and favour a lodgment on that part of the fort that faces the eastern shore'. Provided that the three ships could anchor, Captain Hervey considered that El Morro could quite easily be attacked 'on its N. angle' without risk of exposure to other fire. 'The batteries on the western side of the entrance do not open till the fort bears $S \frac{1}{2} W$. or S. a little easterly; the starboard not open till it is $SE \frac{1}{2} E$.'

To Hervey, the strength of the El Morro fortress had been overrated. He did not think that it commanded the town 'at all' and had very little influence on the harbour. He felt that the key commanding position was on the south side. To him, the western side appeared 'a very fine coast, cleared and very easy for a descent, level to the town' and with no obstruction to any of its approaches. He was therefore of opinion that 'an attack that way could not fail of success'.

On 10 June, the day following his report to Commodore Keppel, Captain Hervey sent a copy of it to Sir George Pocock, clearly angling for a change of venue. If, as he said, a new attack to westward was being contemplated, he hoped to be 'down thereabouts too to be of use'. As the Spaniards had immobilised their ships inside the harbour and had sunk three of them across the boom, they could not get out to attack the British fleet. So Captain Hervey felt that Admiral Pocock would probably now move his squadron nearer to Lord Albemarle; or else that he would remain where he was 'to superintend that *descent*'. In which case, Captain Hervey expressed a wish 'to command *that*', under the Admiral's direction. With a temerity unusual for a junior captain to his admiral, Hervey continued:

Far more large ships must be sent here or you will soon knock up the seamen of these with the many repeated duties they are necessarily required upon. The *Temple*, *Culloden*, *Cambridge*, and those heavy sailing ships will do

for this work ... and I think you may let me command
that descent under [your] flag without any offence to
Barker [Captain Barker of *Culloden*] if he comes up
here.... I wish to be of especial use and in service;
landing cannon, stores, tents, and cutting roads etc.
other people will execute as well. I do not mean this by
way of wanting to get away *from here*, but really to be
in more service, for on the contrary, I have met with all
distinction from Mr Keppel, and who has made more
merit with my services than they desired [deserved?]
and Lord Albemarle thanked me for advancing the
march of their army so much sooner than they could
otherwise have done had I not immediately drove the
enemy from that very strong position on the River
Coximar.

Having clearly listed his qualifications for the Admiral's
eye, Captain Hervey ended with an indirect crack at Sir
Charles Knowles: 'I wish the people in England would
never pretend to give directions where to land, as their intelligence is generally wrong, and in this case I am sure the
west coast is best.'

At that moment, neither Commodore Keppel nor Lord
Albemarle was in favour of using warships to attack El
Morro. Apart from his overall concentration on besieging
the fortress from the land on the east side, Lord Albemarle
was already intent on his scheme to send Colonel Howe with
a body of men to Admiral Pocock at Chorera; while Commodore Keppel feared that Captain Hervey's 'three heavy
ships' could come under intense fire from the fort of La
Punta, commanding the entrance to Havana harbour on the
west side. Apparently Admiral Pocock felt that Captain
Hervey's scheme was 'worth trying', and a detailed recon-
naissance of the north side of El Morro was decreed.

Consequently, on the night of 11 June soundings there were taken by the masters of the *Marlborough, Cambridge* and *Culloden*. They found enough water within a cable's length of El Morro to anchor a ship of the line. It was too dark to gauge the height of the fortress walls above them, so that they had no idea whether a ship's guns could be elevated high enough to damage the fortress itself. There was thus a big element of risk in Captain Hervey's plan of assault. Even so, 'it was decided' that as the land batteries opened fire on El Morro a simultaneous naval attack on the fortress should be made; that the *Dragon, Cambridge* and *Marlborough* should be the ships employed, with the *Stirling Castle* in reserve; and that Captain Hervey should command this bombarding force, 'under the general direction of Commodore Keppel'.

Earlier that day, Admiral Pocock had carried out his decisive operation against the castle of Chorera, with marines from the *Culloden, Stirling Castle, Dublin, Defiance, Marlborough, Nottingham* and *Devonshire*. Four ships of the line were left cruising off the entrance to Havana harbour while the *Belleisle, Echo* and *Cerberus*, the sloop *Bonetta* and the cutter *Lurcher* closed in to bombard the castle. At 11 a.m. the marines landed and by noon they had captured the castle. They found there six pieces of cannon, which they dismounted. On 12 June in a note to Lord Albemarle from the *Namur*, Sir George Pocock expressed himself satisfied. 'I landed the marines yesterday at noon . . . on this side and the shore [is] very favourable.' So much so that he intended to anchor 'some of the men-of-war and all the victuallers, etc.'

The mammoth labours of troops and seamen before El Morro delayed Colonel Howe's departure to join Sir George Pocock's forces at Chorera. But on 15 June 800 marines and 2,000 light infantry and grenadiers under his command landed without opposition to occupy the area around the

mouth of the Chorera river. This operation had been designed as a diversion to draw off some of the Spanish troops
from El Morro, but it proved of far greater importance than
originally envisaged. By it the British army acquired its main
source of fresh water; and the British navy found much better
anchorage at Chorera than at Coximar. (For his part in this
exercise, Colonel Howe also was made a brigadier.)

Mante elaborates:

> Thus, the enemy's communications between town and
> country were cut and their attention perpetually div-
> ided. Posts were secured at St Lazaro and at Snuff [?]
> mills on the river Chorera ... to protect the parties em-
> ployed in taking in water ... for the use of the army on
> the east side of the town. [Major-General Keppel recon-
> noitred El Morro] with as much accuracy as the nature
> of the thick woods surrounding it would permit. It was
> with difficulty discovered that the parapet of the fort was
> thin, and all of masonry, and this discovery showed the
> necessity of erecting a battery against it, as near as the
> cover of the woods would permit.

The work of erecting the batteries continued under gruelling conditions. Under burning sun or tropical downpour
the sappers and seamen laboured on. Colonel Mackellar observes that the landing of the stores was carried out 'with
great diligence by the fleet'. In his report to Admiral Pocock
of 13 June Commodore Keppel tells him that to date the navy
had landed 'ten twenty-four-pounders, four howitzers, six
twelve-pounders, and some smaller ones'. But these, he considered, were the least of their difficulties. '... the roads and
distance to draw them will, I fear, knock us up, but we must
try and take our chance.' Mante continues:

> Cannon and mortars, some of which weighed several

tons, had to be unloaded from the ships, landed through the surf at Coximar, then dragged several miles over rough roads surfaced with logs to the site of the batteries. The ammunition for the guns also had to be carried by soldiers and seamen from the beach to the gun positions. Moreover, the material needed for building fortifications—timber, and earth to fill sandbags—had to be moved into place by hand.

On 14 June Commodore Keppel sent Admiral Pocock a letter informing him that Lord Albemarle intended sending Brigadier Carleton to 'the Governor of Havana' (Don Juan de Prado) with a flag of truce, if the Admiral could transport him. This was to barter a Spanish merchant, Don Mirales (taken prisoner with his ship on the way to Havana), for the captain of the *Lurcher* and the first lieutenant of the *Richmond* who had been captured in the dense woods near El Morro. Commodore Keppel pointed out that as Don Mirales was the Admiral's prisoner, 'the compliment of giving him his liberty' was the Admiral's due. He hoped that, when it was known who the two naval officers were, they might be 'treated accordingly'. In the same letter he enumerated atrocities committed on about seventy British seamen in the woods. This was the third time he had informed the Admiral that Lord Albemarle intended using Don Mirales as a hostage.

On 15 June Sir George Pocock took action on his Commodore's information and wrote a formal letter of complaint to the Governor:

> Sir, It having come to my knowledge that several of the seamen belonging to His Britannic Majesty's fleet under my command have been barbarously treated when taken prisoners by the Spaniards, even such as have been met without arms, I take occasion to represent to Your

Excellency as entirely unbecoming the usage that ought to subsist between two Christian nations that unfortunately are now at war and have carried it on, as far as such a state would admit of, agreeable to the principles of humanity; and I hope we shall never deviate from the constant practise of civilized countries, which I shall make the rule of my actions, during the unhappy state we are embarked in, and I trust Your Excellency is in the same way of thinking with me.

In the same lofty vein he mentioned that the two naval officers were missing, but that he had no doubt that if brought into town they would be treated as befitted 'officers serving in His Britannic Majesty's Navy'. He ended by saying that Don Mirales, 'a merchant of Havana', had asked to be released on parole to mediate for the officers concerned.

Hardly surprisingly, Don Juan de Prado refused to receive Brigadier Carleton and Captain Elphinston as the British Admiral's envoys. The Admiral's letter was never delivered to him, and the fate of the two naval officers remained unknown.

8

Attack from the Sea

For fourteen days, the sun shone down mercilessly on the British forces struggling to set up the batteries before El Morro and on La Cabaña, baking dry everything beneath it, including the fascines. With each day that passed, the hardships sustained by British troops and seamen increased. As Mante records:

> There being no river or even spring near them, it was necessary to bring their water from a great distance; and so scanty and precarious was this supply that they were obliged to have recourse to water from the ships. [In fact, water had to be transported by sea from Chorera, landed through the surf, and thereafter distributed to the troops.] Roads [had] to be cut through thick woods... artillery to be dragged for a vast way over a rough rocky shore. Several of the men on these services dropped down dead with heat, thirst and fatigue. But such was the spirit of the English and such the happy and perfect unanimity that subsisted between the land and sea departments that no difficulty or distress could slacken for a moment the operations.... Batteries were, in spite of all obstacles, raised against El Morro and against the ships in the harbour.

The Spaniards subjected the working parties to a ceaseless bombardment from the warships in the harbour and the guns of El Morro, to which the British bomb-vessels replied at night with shells on El Morro and the city. At last

Carleton's forces mounted their heavy mortars on La Cabaña and from there directed such a heavy fire on the Spanish fleet that for a time they drove it from the harbour's eastern end.

With Don Luis de Velasco in command of the garrison of El Morro, the morale of its defenders had risen. He was intent on keeping his men as fit as possible, every four to six days replacing his garrison with a fresh one, recruited from the town. The fortress mounted about seventy guns, and Valesco's garrison consisted of 300 infantry, fifty seamen and an equal number of gunners, and 300 negro labourers. His first move was to wall up the gate of the castle so that no one could get in from the outside except by hanging ladders; his next was to keep up a continuous fire; and his third was to urge the authorities to 'sally out', to attack the works which the British were trying with such difficulty to put up. His fearless example put new heart into the garrison, which soon began to take in reinforcements from the interior. Overall, he adhered to de Hevia's strategy, which was to drag out the battle for El Morro for as long as possible until 'the ravages of tropical disease' or the advent of the hurricane season, or both, should force the British to lift the siege.

Food as well as water was in short supply for the British forces, as Sir George Pocock wrote to Commodore Keppel on 15 June: 'The New York bread and the provisions on board the transports has turned out unfit for service.... I do not know of any victualler that has butter on board. The *Coronation* has mostly bread, and oil in lieu of butter, therefore, have sent her up to you.' The Admiral was despondent, too, about the sailors' rum ration. 'I should have no objection to the seamen at work on shore having [a] double allowance of rum, if we could spare it, but there is so little in the fleet that we must soon go to short allowance if a supply does not arrive from Jamaica; therefore, they must not have it at present.'

Though on 17 June Lord Albemarle reported that 'the great battery is very near and I should imagine when finished will do very well', his messages to Sir George Pocock continued equally sombre in tone. 'We go on very slowly, hot and rainy weather by turns, very bad roads, no earth to make our batteries of. . . .' In this letter he voiced what Commodore Keppel had already reported, that 'the Governor has sent to Santiago de Cuba, the Matanzas, and Port au Prince for all those troops at those places to join him.' He urged the Admiral to send 'a ship and frigate to guard the south side of the island [which] would probably intercept those troops and prevent any reinforcements getting in.' He too sighed for Sir Jeffery Amherst's troops. 'I wish the North Americans were arrived, we want them much and Governor Lyttelton's blacks.'

On 20 June, from his headquarters at Coximar, Lord Albemarle sent Sir George Pocock an S.O.S.

> Dear Sir,
>
> We are so distressed for water with this dry weather that unless you are so good as to assist us, I don't know what we shall do. Part of four brigades water upon our left of the wood and are cannonaded the whole day, the rest and working parties to this time have been supplied with rain water upon the beach. If you could send us water in casks to the landing place, I would order a guard upon it to prevent the casks being spoilt. . . .'

Despite his understatement, the urgency of his message is obvious. The horrors of the lack of water are described by Mante in his account of the siege.

Following Sir George Pocock's decision to mount a naval attack on El Morro to coincide with Lord Albemarle's assault on it with land batteries, Commodore Keppel informed the

Admiral on 22 June that he had signalled the *Cambridge* and
Marlborough 'to come up'. (It will be remembered that Captain Hervey in the *Dragon* was to command this bombarding
force of three ships—*Dragon, Cambridge* and *Marlborough*—
with the *Stirling Castle* in reserve.) The Commodore further
informed his chief that Lord Albemarle's Grand Battery was
almost ready and that Lord Albemarle hoped to 'gun his
battery' that Saturday. Thereafter, if the wind and general
projects were favourable, the Commodore would send the
ships 'to cooperate with the army in beginning the attack'.

From his despatch, it is clear that Sir George Pocock too
had had misgivings about the success of the venture before
El Morro.

> I stated all yours and my doubts to Captain Hervey,
> who is fond of the project, and he proposed by way of
> clearing the matter to proceed with a fresh breeze in the
> *Dragon*, take the soundings and survey the batteries with-
> out anchoring, and if he finds the ship's guns likely to do
> service, he will make his report, which I shall immediate-
> ly send to you, and if it is such as to encourage the ships
> attacking, I shall be in readiness, if it meets your appro-
> bation. If I hear nothing to the contrary from you,
> Captain Hervey in the *Dragon* shall make the experiment
> the moment the wind offers. He is, as soon as he is con-
> vinced, to get out of shot as soon as possible. Whatever
> alteration you would please have in this operation, I
> shall endeavour to have done in the manner you like
> best. . . .

Apparently the Admiral saw nothing to alter in these
arrangements, as he noted in his journal on 23 June: 'At
$\frac{1}{2}$ past 4 p.m. Commodore Keppel hoisted a standard at his
main-top gallant-mast, which I answered, on which the
Cambridge and *Marlborough* made sail to the eastward, they

George, 3rd Earl of Albemarle
by Francis Cotes, 1765 (pastel)

Major-General the Hon. William Keppel
by Francis Cotes, 1764 (pastel)

Rear-Admiral the Hon. Augustus Keppel
by Francis Cotes, 1765 (pastel)

THE CAPTURE OF HAVANA, 13ᵗʰ August, 1762

by the BRITISH FORCES under the Command of the Earl of Albemarle and Sʳ Geo: Pocock.

from a contemporary print

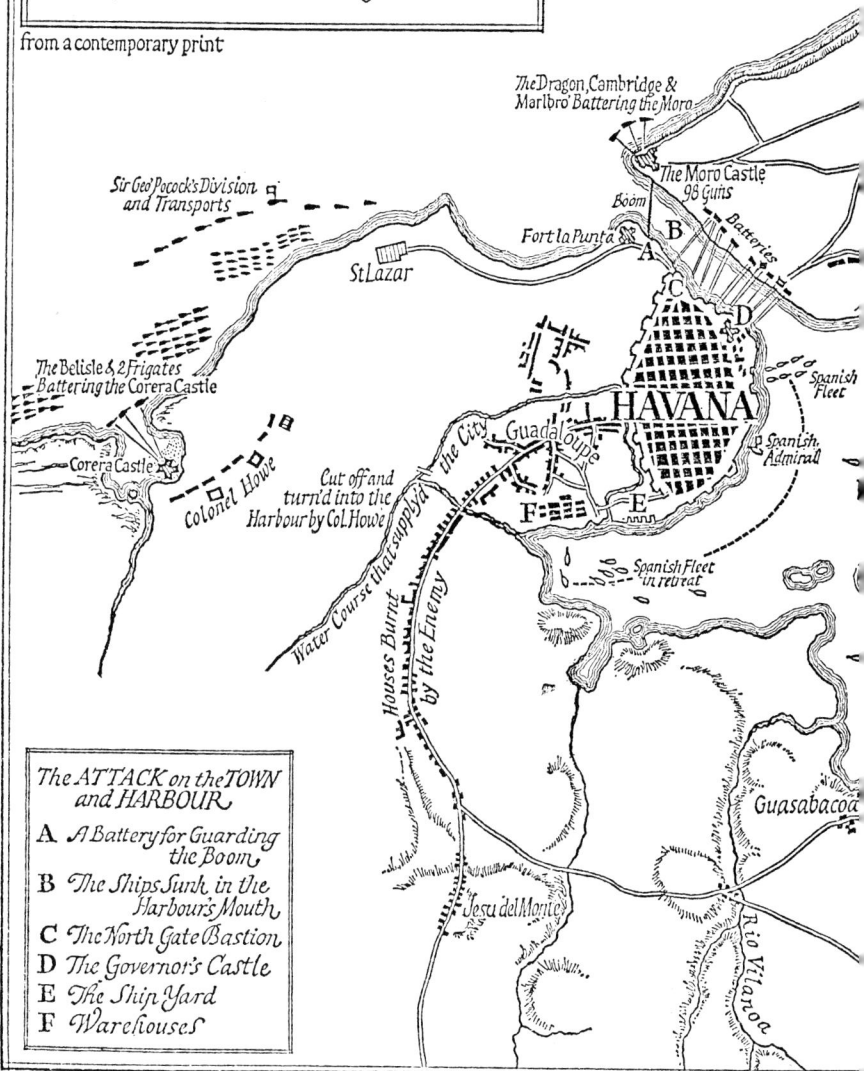

The Dragon, Cambridge & Marlbro' Battering the Moro

Sir Geo Pocock's Division and Transports

The Moro Castle 98 Guns

Boom

Fort la Punta

A B

St Lazar

C

D

The Belisle & 2 Frigates Battering the Corera Castle

Spanish Fleet

Corera Castle

Colonel Howe

Cut off and turn'd into the Harbour by Col. Howe

The City

Guadaloupe

HAVANA

Spanish Admirall

Water Course that supplyd the City

Houses Burnt by the Enemy

F

E

Spanish Fleet in retreat

Guasabacoa

Jesu del Monte

Rio Vilanoa

The ATTACK on the TOWN and HARBOUR

A A Battery for Guarding the Boom
B The Ships Sunk in the Harbour's Mouth
C The North Gate Bastion
D The Governor's Castle
E The Ship Yard
F Warehouses

Map of the Capture of Havana, 13 August 1762
(with acknowledgements—as used also in Sir Hugh Thomas's *Cuba*)

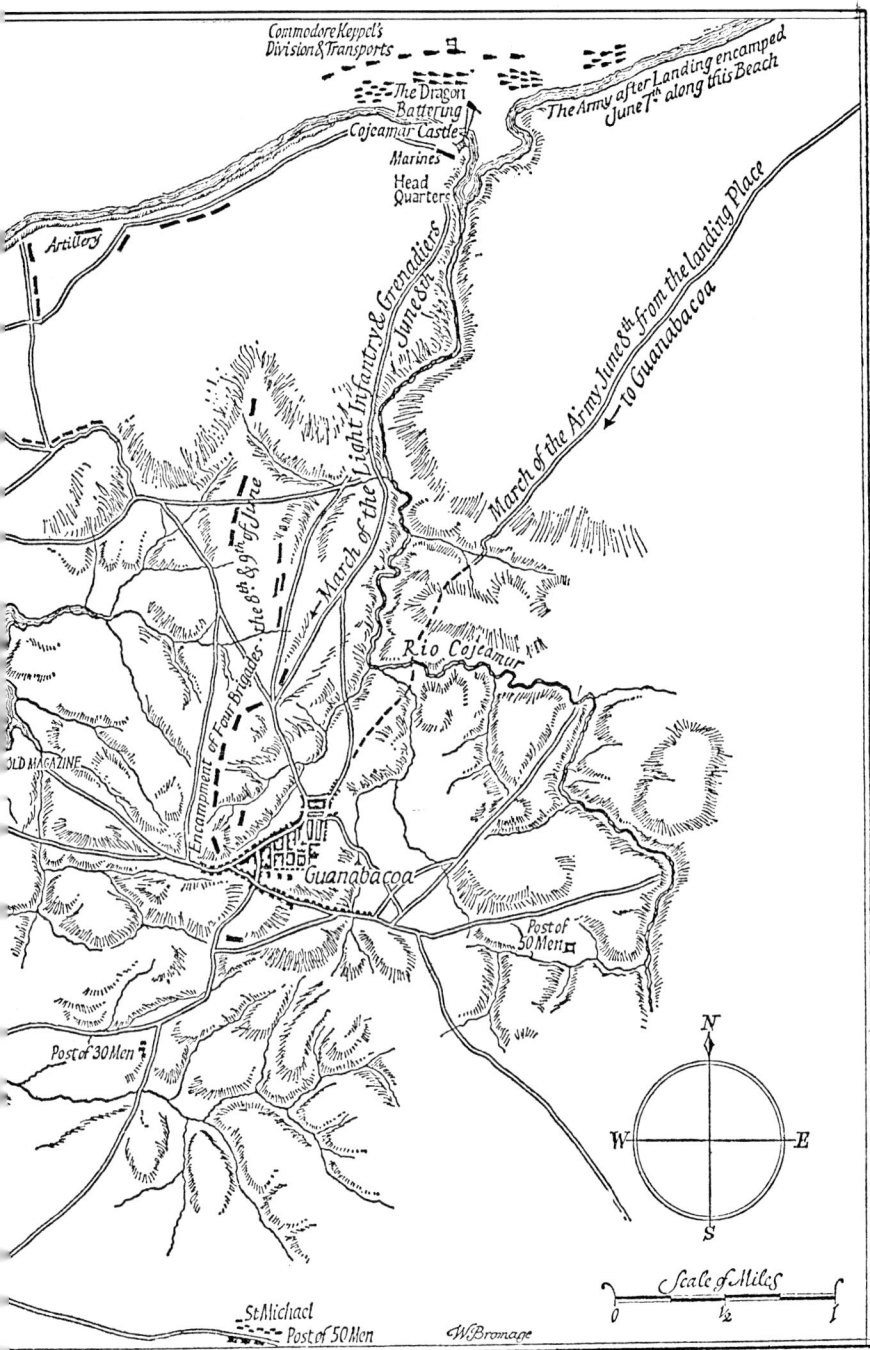

Commodore Keppel's
Division & Transports

The Army after Landing encamped
June 7th along this Beach

The Dragon
Battering
Cojcamar Castle

Marines

Head
Quarters

Artillery

March of the Army June 8th from the landing Place
to Guanabacoa

March of the Light Infantry & Grenadiers
June 8th

March of the 6th 8 9th of June

Encampment of Four Brigades

Rio Cojeamur

OLD MAGAZINE

Guanabacoa

Post of
30 Men

Post of 30 Men

N

W   E

S

St. Michael
Post of 50 Men

W. Bromage

Scale of Miles

0   ½   1

'A View of the Market Place in the City of Havana'

'The Breach of the Moro Castle by Storm—30 July 1762'
after the painting by Dominic Serres

Commodore Keppel, in *Valiant*, leading the British fleet into Havana harbour, 15 August 1762

being intended to attack El Morro Castle....' Keppel
acknowledged this signal in his journal of 28 June:

> Sir George Pocock gave me orders to direct Captain
> Hervey to take charge of that service with the *Dragon*,
> *Cambridge* and *Marlborough*. I gave Captain Hervey and
> the other captains orders to this purpose and to prepare
> their ships accordingly.

But even before the main bombardment began, the *Dragon*
lost an anchor.

Under the command of Major-General William Keppel,
at daybreak on 1 July, four land batteries, consisting of twelve
24-pounder cannon, nine 13-inch and 10-inch mortars, and
twenty-six royal mortars, opened fire on the land sides of the
fortress of El Morro, expecting that at the same moment
Hervey's three ships of the line, with the *Stirling Castle* in the
van, would start bombarding El Morro from the west.

To draw the enemy's fire, the *Stirling Castle* was to sail
along the north side of the fortress, while the *Dragon*, *Cambridge* and *Marlborough* anchored under it. Thereafter 'the
Stirling Castle was to stand off El Morro and support the
other three ships during the bombardment.' This manoeuvre
was added by the Commodore himself, who elaborated: 'The
Stirling Castle I had added to the three other ships, intending
her to proceed first in order to draw the fire of the enemy
while the other ships were placing themselves and then to
lead out and hold herself ready for any service she might be
wanted for.' But later on 1 July he noted: 'The *Stirling Castle*
did not get ahead that morning.'

There was very little wind, and the *Stirling Castle*, supposed to be leading, fell steadily behind the other three ships.
A puzzled Captain Hervey sent an officer to find out why
she did not set more sail and take her position in the van.
The daunting answer came back that Captain Campbell had

sent ashore most of his ship's sails, yards and booms. Sometimes before an action a ship's spars were taken down to protect them from damage, but on this occasion Captain Hervey had a clear view of the *Stirling Castle*'s main and sprit sails 'in place, but furled'. Despite his repeated signals to Captain Campbell to set them, furled they remained.

As a result, the *Stirling Castle* fell further and further behind and it was not till 9.10 a.m. that the first ship, the *Cambridge*, anchored alongside El Morro and began to bombard it. Twenty minutes later, the *Dragon*, followed immediately by the *Marlborough*, also anchored alongside the fortress and began to fire. Thick smoke obscured the space between ships and fortress but, as it cleared, two factors became obvious. The British fire was doing very little damage to the solid stone foundations of El Morro; and, although the Spanish guns were set too high to hit the hulls of the ships, they were doing great damage to the British rigging and masts.

The trail of disaster continued. Having already lost one anchor when weighing, before ever the bombardment started, almost immediately after engaging El Morro Captain Hervey lost a second, and the *Dragon* went aground. 'Within minutes of engaging El Morro, the rigging of the *Cambridge* was shattered, several of her guns dismounted, and her captain (Goostrey) killed.' (Immediately on receiving the signal of the captain's injury, Commodore Keppel, watching the bombardment from the *Orford*, sent Captain Lindsay of the *Trent* to take over command of the *Cambridge*.) By half past eleven, Captain Hervey had sent the Commodore two messages, one written in pencil on a set of public signals issued for use in the bombardment. Both notified him that the *Dragon* was aground, though still firing, and asked him to send a frigate to tow her away. The pencilled message was signed: 'Often duller, Ever Yours, A. Hervey.'

At last the *Stirling Castle* arrived on the scene, and was

ordered to drop a heavy anchor 'about three cable's length off the starboard bow of the *Dragon*' and 'to pass a heavy cable to her' so that she could be kedged away from El Morro. This command, too, Captain Campbell ignored. He sent in a boat with a light anchor and small hawser, which was not heavy enough to kedge away the *Dragon*; so that in the end Captain Hervey had to save his ship by his own exertions— as this extract from his log-book of 1 July testifies:

The *Stirling Castle* not dropping her anchor, we were obliged to carry out our stream anchor (the only one we had left) with a stream cable and hawser and dropped it without us, continuing the whole time to engage the Castle, whose fire also was very quick and heavy. We hove a great strain. At noon began to stave the water, wine and spirits abaft, and ditto pumped it out, as also to throw some junk overboard and get several stores into flat boats....

At 11.30 a.m., from the *Orford*, Commodore Keppel informed Admiral Pocock that he had directed Captain Hervey not to keep 'the 80-gun ship' (*Cambridge*) before El Morro longer than was necessary. 'I should believe that the height of El Morro is too great, and that it is right for all to come away with the night.' At 2 p.m. he confirmed that Captain Hervey and the *Marlborough* were 'in safety'. He believed that all the Admiral's officers had behaved well, and recommended the first lieutenant of the *Cambridge* 'to take over command of the ship'. He praised the fearless behaviour of Captain Lindsay, transferred in battle from his own ship, the *Trent*, to take over the *Cambridge*.

Later that day Sir George Pocock approved the Commodore's recommendations, and the lifting of the naval assault on El Morro. Thereafter, according to Keppel's journal: 'The ships got off from El Morro having suffered in their

masts, sails, and rigging and lost several men, particularly the
Cambridge. They stood to leeward and joined the Admiral.'

The casualties resulting from Captain Hervey's hazardous
plan of assault were 192 officers and men, killed and
wounded. Yet, even though Mackellar admits that the
three ships concerned did not inflict much damage on the
fortress above them, he insists that 'they still did us (the land
forces) a considerable service in taking up the enemy's attention for that time which gained us a superiority in the
number of guns.'

Captain Hervey's letter to Commodore Keppel of 3 July
from the *Dragon* is a model of self-complacency with a streak
of vindictiveness running through it:

> Dear Sir,
>
> I have sent my sloop up for the sick people and tent.
> I am very happy to find we have given satisfaction and
> that we were of such use to the General as Lord
> Albemarle's letter flatters me with. As to the *Stirling
> Castle*, I think the Admiral seems to have seen enough
> to be a judge how far it is right to trust *such* a ship to
> *such* a commander, and I would not write a complaint as
> you seemed so merciful to him, but I believe his officers
> will represent his conduct.
>
> I beg my compliments to my Lord and the General.
> I hope you are all well and will soon be masters of El
> Morro. I shall wait on you in a day or two to pay my
> respects to yourself. . . .
>
>   Yr. faithful and obedient servant
>   A. HERVEY.

Captain Hervey made his point. A month later, Captain
Campbell was tried and convicted by court-martial, and
dismissed the Service.

9
The Ditch

With never-failing good manners, Lord Albemarle wrote from the *Orford* to thank Sir George Pocock for the Navy's assistance in the siege.

> Dear Sir,
>   Your ships have done incomparably well. I am afraid the 80-gun ship has suffered greatly. They have drawn much fire from our batteries; *the great one* [Grand Battery] is battering a breach, and the wall tumbles very fast; we shall soon make a practicable breach....

To this Sir George Pocock sent an immediate answer in the same vein.

> My dear Lord,
>   It gave me much pleasure to find that our ships were so serviceable to [the] acting of your Grand Battery against El Morro, with the likelihood of your making very soon a practicable breach.... The *Cambridge* was somewhat in trouble, but that will be amply repaid in the same loss from our friends upon the hill near El Morro. We shall be always at your service for the common cause....

The British besieging forces increased the intensity of their assault, opening up a new battery on the east side, and incorporating into it four 32-pound naval guns removed from the *Orford* and *Temple*. Commodore Keppel also pressed the Admiral to let him have another 'ship or two...to cut fascines'. But on 2 July there is an alarming entry in Mackellar's journal:

> Our batteries continued their fire with great success and beat down the front attacked as fast as could be wished or expected, particularly the 8-gun battery; but unhappily about noon we were obliged to slacken that battery, being in danger of catching fire from the constant fire kept up, (and) the dryness of the fascines, having no rain for 14 days. . . .

With no water at hand, the dirt with which the British troops tried to smother the flames itself ignited, and the Grand Battery was destroyed. 'Thus', Mackellar recorded, '17 days' labour of 500–600 men, and which must have let us into the fort in a few days, was now baffled and to do over again.'

The Spaniards took full advantage of this slackening of enemy fire, remounting a number of guns with which they bombarded the British working and fire-fighting parties. Again and again the British sappers repaired their batteries, opened them up, and had them knocked out again. The Grand Battery was brought back into partial use; but in the afternoon of 11 July the merlons again caught fire, the flames spreading from right to left. This time, Mackellar notes, 'the whole was irreparably consumed'.

Meanwhile, the Navy continued to supply invaluable help. On 5 and 6 July 400 marines were brought to the siege of El Morro from Brigadier Howe's corps at Chorera, and another 300 seamen landed from their ships. They were put to making 20,000 sandbags from old sails and biscuit-bags, and several 'working tools' for the artillery park. To protect the gun crews from the enemy's fire, they began to make several hundred 'mantelets' from pieces of old junk and cordage. But 'the men in general fell down with fevers and fluxes' and the health of the besiegers deteriorated hourly.

Mante declared that from 1 July onwards the hardships endured by British soldiers and seamen before El Morro had become 'almost insupportable'. Even by that time, 5,000 soldiers and 3,000 sailors were laid low 'with various distempers', while a want of fresh provisions retarded their recovery. Thirst was the worst of all the agonies they endured.

[Thirst] soon caused the tongue to swell, extend itself within the lips and become black as in a state of mortification; then the whole frame became a prey to the most excruciating agonies, till death at length intervened, and gave the unhappy sufferer relief. In this way hundreds resigned themselves to eternity. A great number fell prey to a putrid fever. From the appearance of perfect health 3 or 4 short hours robbed them of existence. Many there were who endured a loathsome disease for days, nay weeks together, living in a state of putrefaction, their bodies full of vermin and almost eaten away before the spark of life was extinguished. The carrion crows of the country kept constantly hovering over the graves which rather hid than buried the dead, and frequently scratched away the scanty earth, leaving in every mangled corpse a spectacle of unspeakable loathsomeness and terror to those who, by being engaged in the same enterprise, were exposed to the same fate. Hundreds of carcasses were seen floating on the ocean. Yet all these accumulated horrors damped not the ardour of the survivors. Used to conquest and to brave every kind of danger, every one exerted himself with such a particular aim of victory as if the whole enterprise depended on a single arm. . . .

Amid this purgatory of human suffering, Mante praised the steadiness of the commanding officers. On 6 July Commodore

Keppel reported to Admiral Pocock that both his brothers were sick.

Six days later, in the *Centurion*, Sir James Douglas appeared with the Jamaica convoy, which he was escorting home. He came to drop 'some hundreds of negroes' whom Lord Albemarle had bought as labourers. Mante voiced the disappointment that it was Sir James's convoy and not Sir Jeffery Amherst's long-awaited fleet that had arrived. 'A much more useful fleet was expected from North America ...a thousand impatient and languishing looks were cast out for it; but all in vain....' Nevertheless '20 guns were mounted by the 16th...[and] all the artillery ammunition and stores...'. Mante also praised the efforts of the 1,500 negroes involved as behaving 'in a manner that does them infinite honour'. Tremendous efforts were made to repair the merlons at night 'with logs of cedar, which they covered with nets of thick rope in order to secure themselves from the splinter'. (Lord Albemarle's purchase of negro labour had been cheap: 5 pence a day each, instead of the usual price of 15 pence.)

With Sir James Douglas's arrival, Lord Albemarle had to prepare a despatch for Sir James to take home to Lord Egremont (Secretary of State), reporting progress on the siege. Already on 8 July he had expressed his fears to Sir George Pocock that Sir James might arrive before he had a decisive victory to announce. 'I must write by him, and I cannot tell them at home positively that I shall take El Morro, tho I have no doubt about it myself.' So he told Sir George that he would prepare 'a sort of journal to this time, with very few comments upon it'. This he did, on 13 July.

> We are pushing the siege of El Morro Fort with the utmost vigour.... We have open in different batteries twenty-four guns, some of which are within 300 yards of

the wall; four large mortars, and many royals are constantly bombarding the fort, which makes an obstinate
and gallant defence, but with so superior a fire we hope
soon to ruin their defences and make a lodgment on their
covered way and from thence to batter in breach.

Then he had to be more realistic.

The increasing sickness of the troops, the intense heat of
the weather, and the approaching rainy season are circumstances which prevent my being too sanguine as to
our future success against the town, particularly as we
have no news of the American reinforcements, but I
greatly depend on the courage and firmness of the army
under my command and the powerful assistance which I
receive from Sir George Pocock and Commodore
Keppel.

At that point, resolute as he was, Lord Albemarle may
have wondered whether the siege of El Morro was worth
continuing. For by then Commodore Keppel had no doubt
told him (as he had told Admiral Pocock on 8 July) that he
had had a letter from England which informed him that 'the
Duc de Choiseul has again offered Lord Bute to enter into
[peace] negotiation, and it is believed his Lordship has
accepted it.'

The shortage of men through sickness before El Morro
was by now so acute that Albemarle was forced to withdraw General Eliott's corps from Guanabocoa to reinforce
them. The sailors were called in again to help, and on 13 July
Commodore Keppel complained to Admiral Pocock that
'this cursed Jamaica convoy not only lands rum but seduces
the seamen away, both from the King's ships and transports. I wish they were gone with all my heart.' In the same

letter he refers indirectly to his own sickness: 'I am much easier since bleeding.'

Despite their heroic performance it seemed only a matter of days before dysentery and yellow fever would compel the British forces to withdraw altogether from Havana.

In his 'journal' to Lord Egremont of 13 July Lord Albemarle had referred to the enemy's 'covered way'. For some time Major-General Keppel (who had been confirmed in his rank on 10 July) and his engineers had been studying the glacis between their batteries and El Morro. They had discovered that it could not be approached in the ordinary way, by digging trenches, as it was of solid stone. Furthermore, the ditch originally referred to by Sir Charles Knowles was, as Thomas Mante had already reported, of 'immense depth' (from fifty-six to sixty-five feet deep; and thirty-five to a hundred and five feet wide). This also was cut out of solid stone. Consequently, the fortress could not be stormed until the assault troops had found a way to get over the glacis and the ditch.

Colonel Mackellar and his engineers now evolved a plan to build 'a line of breastworks and barricades which would run north-west across the surface of the glacis for approximately nine hundred and fifty feet', which meant from the British lines up to the edge of the ditch under the right bastion of the fortress, where it met the sea. To achieve their purpose, 'warships, transports, and army encampments were ransacked for materials to construct this barrier'; working parties of soldiers and seamen were detailed to make gabions, sandbags, wool-packs and mantelets; and bales of cotton from the homegoing West Indies convoy were used 'to provide the basis for much of the construction'.

Although the Spaniards still had two guns mounted on El Morro, the British, with more than twenty guns and a number of mortars in action, had by 17 July successfully silenced the fire from the fortress's right bastion. That night they began to work on their sap. Lord Albemarle ordered a communication trench ('a boyau') to be made all along the seashore, and this was protected by gabions filled with cotton, for want of better material. Despite enemy attempts to disrupt them, by the night of 19 July, working night and day, they had made a lodgment on the covered way under this same bastion. The next day they built a breastwork along the edge of the covered way running parallel with the landward face of El Morro, from which small arms fire could be directed to the top of the fortress's walls. They then dragged up to the main sap eighteen coehorns, one 12-pound and one 24-pound cannon, thus forming a battery opposite the right bastion. (The 12-pounder was to be used to cover the salient angle of the covered way; the 24-pounder was to cover the point where the British intended to breach the wall of the bastion.)

On reaching the covered way, the sappers found that a stone ridge crossed the ditch, keeping out the sea. The top of this was wide enough for a line of men in single file to cross from the covered way to the foot of the right bastion wall. By sinking one mine under the wall at the end of the ridge and another under the covered way, 'to throw the escarpment into the ditch', the engineers decided to form a runway for the assaulting troops to cross. On 20 July the army sappers, 'reinforced by seamen who were ex-tin miners', crossed the stone ridge, as planned. They lost four men 'to Spanish small arms fire' but continued mining the wall of the right bastion; and mining under the 'counterscarp' was begun at the same time.

To quote Mante:

It now became visible to the Governor of the Havana that . . . it must speedily be reduced. He therefore made

every preparation for a strong sortie, and every en-
couragement was offered to the country militia mulat-
toes and negroes that could operate on such bigoted
minds; such as prayers, bulls, pardons and absolutions.
The circumstances were now become desperate...one
decisive blow was their only resource.

By [2 a.m. on] 22 July the English miners had
penetrated about 18 feet under the face of the bastion of
the Moro. The engineers, fearing it [the sap] should be
taken in flank from the town had directed it should turn
off from the glacis and be carried along the height, from
whence...the bare rock slopes to the sea on one side
and to the harbour on the other.

The Spaniards made three determined attempts 'to destroy the British mines and to spike the guns bombarding
El Morro', all of which were repulsed. One group crossed
the harbour and landed between El Morro and La Cabaña,
but were checked by the 3rd Battalion of the Royal Americans and driven back to their boats. A second was directed
against the British miners and sappers, but they ran out of
ammunition and had to withdraw. A third landed at the foot
of La Cabaña and tried to assault the British guns covering
the harbour.

Brigadier Carleton showed Captain Dixon, engineer for
the night, the only spot where 'the sap might be carried on
with ease and safety and when made would command the
entrance of the ditch and front'. This was agreed. Mante
continues:

At approach of day a sergeant and 12 men were detached. Their orders were to make no noise and to ob-
serve well the work, the nature of the communications
with the body of the fort and if possible the state of the

garrison ... they descended a ladder placed in a confined hold of the rock to the edge and level of the sea, from whence they mounted a longer ladder and endeavoured to get to the top of the parapet. These ladders had been placed before by 2 engineers ... large stones were thrown down upon them ... [and] the 3rd man had scarcely reached the top of the ladder when about 12 Spaniards ... started up and gave the alarm. The sergeant returned but was sent back immediately.... The alarm bell rang on the Moro. Reveille was beat by drummers (although not yet dawn) for which the English on the glacis could see no cause. Soon after shots rang out and heavy musketry heard.

That dark night a body of 2500 Spaniards had crossed the harbour in silence. Carleton had ordered patroles every $\frac{1}{2}$ hour but neglect of this precaution afforded the Spaniards the opportunity of concealing themselves among the shrubs at the foot of the hills till the dawn of day, when the tolling of the morning bells was to have been the signal for attack. But it was, fortunately for the besiegers, precipitated by the alarm given from the Moro.

The English, engaged in repairing their batteries, threw down their tools and ran to arms. Dixon and Williams batteries were nearest the harbour and were covered by about 30 men each. [They] advanced into the wood nearer the harbour. Lt. Col. Stuart 90th [Regiment] commanded, [and] his men were placed behind some fascines, which had been thrown there for other purposes, and an abati[s] of a prickly West India shrub, called by botanists 'the Prickly Pear of Ficoides'.

Joined by others, they manoeuvred in the wood and Brigadier Carleton, after clearing the woods and turning short to the right, in order to gain the flank of the

Spaniards, ... marched in file directly to a rock which,
sloping gently to the land, covered the English from the
floating batteries of the Spaniards, as well as those of the
town ... the ground back to the Spanish redoubt term-
inated in a precipice to the harbour ... but towards the
Moro the ground slopes gently and easily to the harbour
and here the Spanish landed and ascended.

Mante observes that 'the English received them with their
usual steadiness' but that some men were killed and wounded
at 'Stuart's' and 'Henry's' posts.

The Spaniards made an attempt on the sap but received a galling fire given them by the royal which lasted
about 10 or 15 minutes ... and being taken in flank ...
they were soon driven down the hill in confusion. The
foremost of the runaways seizing on their boats; those
left behind ... called to their friends on the other side,
like people in despair.

The English formed 'a curved line of one single rank upon
the top of the heights—their shot ... galled exceedingly, while
the fire in return ... proved very desultory and unequal.'

As the light became stronger, Brigadier Carleton thought
it prudent to withdraw, as it would expose his men to the
fire of the ships in the harbour, the Punta Fort and the North
Bastion. He got them off the heights before a single cannon-
shot was fired but a party of Spaniards appeared within
musket shot, having passed by the Spanish redoubt, and
Carleton was wounded by a shot which broke his arm. Major
Farmer took command and drove the Spaniards back to the
place they had come from, and posted his men so that they
could fire down in safety into the boats below. Then General
Keppel 'ordered his brigades' and himself marched with the
Royal Americans to pursue the fugitives, most of whom had

regained the opposite bank. A flag of truce was hung out for the burial of the dead (Mante estimates that British casualties were eighty-five men); the firing was then resumed.

By 29 July the mines had been completed and the British were ready to storm El Morro. Lord Albemarle decided first to try to bluff the Spaniards into withdrawing. 'He fired off guns and staged signals, making it appear that an assault was about to begin, but failed to frighten the Spaniards.' When the actual assault began the next day, they made great efforts to stop it. At 2 a.m. on 30 July they sent round small craft to the seaward side of El Morro and attacked the British miners in the ditch 'with grape-shot and musket fire', but the British small-arms fire drove them off. To quote Mackellar:

> About two o'clock in the afternoon the mines were sprung; that in the counterscarp had not a very considerable effect, but that in the bastion, having thrown down a part of both faces, made a breach which the General (Keppel) and Chief Engineer thought practicable, upon which the troops under orders for the assault were ordered to mount, which they did ... and forming very expeditiously upon the top of the breach, soon drove the enemy from every part of the ramparts.

The British army had triumphed at last. Commodore Keppel formed a floating reserve with the *Alcide* (a 'sixty-four') and a number of armed boats, and prepared to use seamen in the assault on El Morro, but his brother, General Keppel, insisted that the attack must remain military. (As the Commodore told the Admiral: 'General Keppel does not choose our seamen to be employed in entering the breach.')

Colonel James Stuart of the 90th Regiment led the British assault force, which was made up of 268 infantrymen and 150 sappers, with 281 men of the 35th Regiment in reserve. 'They rushed El Morro so quickly and in such numbers that

the Spaniards were unable to stop them.' After an hour's
hand-to-hand fighting, during which the British lost fourteen
killed and twenty-eight wounded, the fortress was theirs.

The captain commanding El Morro, Don Luis de Velasco,
was seriously wounded and taken prisoner; and his second-
in-command, the Marques di Gonzales, was killed. The
British put the rest of the Spanish losses at 130 killed, 37
wounded, 326 captured, and 213 men shot or drowned,
attempting to escape to Havana. By 5 p.m. Commodore
Keppel was appealing to the Admiral for the use of the
sloop *Bonetta* to help take off prisoners.

According to the etiquette of the day, Lord Albemarle
wrote at once to Sir George Pocock, as Admiral of the Fleet,
congratulating him 'upon the possession of El Morro'. Sir
George returned an immediate reply, congratulating Lord
Albemarle in identical terms. After this exchange, both paid
spontaneous tributes to Major-General Keppel, 'his officers
and brave men'.

Officers of both the British armed services were united in their
admiration of the heroic example set by El Morro's garrison
commander, Don Luis de Velasco. At his own request,
he was sent across the harbour to be treated for his
wounds by Spanish surgeons; but, as the night was dark,
Lord Albemarle's aide-de-camp was sent with him with instructions that should any difficulty arise the wounded man
should be brought back to Lord Albemarle's own camp, so
that he could be treated 'with all the care and homage that
was due to an officer who, with so much glory, had known
how to uphold his trust and the honour of his Prince's arms'.
All was to no avail, however, as the gallant captain, who was
to become a legend in his country's history, died of his wounds
two days later.

Victory

The town of Havana still remained to be captured, and this now became the objective of British naval and military strategy. 'Parties of British seamen and soldiers had mounted guns on La Cabaña to fire across the harbour entrance into the city. The beachhead at Chorera was expanded eastward and work was begun on the batteries which were to bombard the city and La Punta.' The Spaniards made several unsuccessful attempts to destroy these batteries. Then, on 28 July, two days before the storming of the breach at El Morro, the first division of the long-awaited North American contingent had appeared at Chorera.

The passage of these troops from America to Havana had been dogged by disaster. Five transports carrying 488 New York provincials and members of the 58th Regiment had been captured in the Caicos Passage by a division of Admiral Blénac's squadron, and a frigate and four more transports had been wrecked at the entrance of the Old Bahama Channel. (When this news reached Sir George Pocock, he despatched the indefatigable Captain Elphinston in the *Richmond*, with some transports and sloops, to take off the wrecked crews.) Although this was only a small portion of the expected American force, the arrival of 3,188 healthy men had a great effect on the morale of the British troops. This effect was enhanced by the arrival of more American troops on 2 August.

Leaving General Keppel to form heavy batteries on the shore end of the Cabaña ridge and to train the batteries from

El Morro on to Havana and the fort of La Punta, Lord Albemarle at long last went over to reconnoitre the west side. Sir Charles Knowles later criticised him for not having done this much earlier, as only then did he discover a road leading almost up to the weak defences of Havana. Admittedly it was blocked by abatis and covered by the guns of La Punta, but if (as Sir Charles argued) the Navy had been allowed to bombard La Punta from the sea, the chances were that in the ensuing panic, and with the land forces advancing from Chorera, capitulation would have been inevitable long before. (He ignored the fact that he himself had originally suggested a landing at Coximar and an approach from the north, although on its east side the fortress of El Morro could dominate the harbour and seaboard of Havana until such time as it was subdued.) Spleen may have soured Sir Charles's reception of the news of the victory, as in 1749 he himself had been court-martialled and severely reprimanded for his dilatory tactics in engaging the Spanish fleet in an earlier battle for Havana, before the Treaty of Aix-la-Chapelle. The charge had been brought against him largely through the activities of four of his officers, who detested him. After his court-martial, Sir Charles was challenged by these same four officers to duels in defence of their honour which, they said, he had slandered. He exchanged shots with one of them (Captain Holmes of the *Lennox*), but soon afterwards George II made all duels illegal. Sir Julian Corbett says of Sir Charles:

> He was beyond question a man that made many and bitter enemies and when in command was neither loved nor feared, though he may have been hated. . . .

The criticism of Lord Albemarle may have been invoked primarily by envy of his success where Knowles himself had failed; and also by Lord Albemarle's capacity, despite his military shortcomings, to inspire loyalty and confidence in those who served under him.

On 31 July Lord Albemarle moved his headquarters to Chorera, where the second contingent of American troops arrived on 2 August. The unevenness of the ground to the west of Havana was a major obstacle, but by now Lord Albemarle was convinced that the city must surrender in the face of the Cabaña and El Morro batteries and the new ones that he was completing on its west side. He was therefore chary of wasting further life in an assault. Sir George Pocock solved the problem of the uneven ground by ordering the fleet carpenters to saw up one of his 'prize' frigates for gun platforms. (During the siege of El Morro, Sir George had been active. Concerned as he was to cover the passage of the Jamaica convoy and the American division when it arrived, and also to guard against possible Spanish attack from outlying stations, he had thrown out a chain of frigates to the Bay of Florida; had kept one cruiser squadron to the east off Matanzas, and another to the west to watch the Yucatan Channel; and thereby, along the way, had acquired a number of prizes.)

By 10 August the British had mounted ten mortars, five howitzers and over forty cannon, and were ready to begin their subjugation of Havana. Later that day, Lord Albemarle sent an aide-de-camp under a flag of truce to Governor Don Juan de Prado 'desiring His Excellency to capitulate'. To this demand Don Juan replied that he would defend the town to the last extremity. (His refusal was couched in flowery language, thanking Lord Albemarle for his offer of 'passports for the ladies' and ending up: 'My Lord, I kiss Your Excellency's hand and remain your most attentive and assured servant, Juan de Prado.')

In consequence, at dawn the next day the British batteries opened fire simultaneously on Havana and on the forts of

La Punta and La Fuerza (a small fort at the south-west side of the entrance to the harbour); and now their superiority told. The guns of La Punta were quickly silenced and the fort abandoned, and most of the guns on the city walls were put out of action. Inevitably the walls would soon be breached and the British would storm the city. By 2 p.m. de Prado had decided that his situation was hopeless, and he asked for terms. White flags were hung out on the city walls, and a Spanish officer was sent over to the British lines with a letter to Lord Albemarle requesting a suspension of hostilities for twenty-four hours.

This truce was agreed to by the British Admiral and Commander-in-Chief, but at first the Spaniards would not agree to the terms of surrender. They wanted to retain their ships in the harbour, whereas the British were equally determined to acquire them. Next day Sir George Pocock and Lord Albemarle sent a joint letter to the Governor, threatening to renew hostilities at once, if their terms of capitulation were not met. This time, Don Juan had no option but to surrender, knowing that further defence of Havana was impossible.

On 13 August Mackellar noted in his journal that the capitulation of Havana had been signed and sealed; and the next day he added:

Thus one of the greatest advantages that Britain has gained over an enemy for many years back was now gained in two months time by a handful of troops, who with great firmness bore with many difficulties uncommon in sieges, and under all the disadvantages of an unhealthy climate in the most sickly season. The assistance they received from the sea service can never be sufficiently admired, and it may be safely affirmed that there never subsisted a greater harmony between the sea and land services, nor more public zeal in both, than upon this occasion.

Thomas Mante confirmed his summing up, in practically identical words. And he added this rider:

> Be posterity therefore further informed that during the whole of this siege, there subsisted such a perfect harmony between the land and sea services, with an extraordinary degree of goodwill in the inferior officers and common men, to execute the orders of their Admiral and General, that both owed their success to such patriotic endeavours.

The British terms of capitulation were strict.

> The city of Havana and its environs were surrendered to the British, together with all military equipment, public records, merchantmen and warships in the harbour, public moneys, and city warehouses with their contents.

Thereafter, the victors made generous concessions to the pride of their defeated enemy. From the Marques del Real Transporte downwards, Spanish soldiers and sailors were accorded honours of war and were to be repatriated back to Spain in British ships. Officers were allowed to take their money and effects with them; garrisons were to march out with drums beating and full military honours (but had to leave their military chests behind). As 'by a mere accident' the former Viceroy of Peru and Don Diego Taveres, Major-General of the King of Spain's forces, happened to be in Havana at the outbreak of hostilities, they were to be conveyed back to Spain 'in a manner suitable to the rank dignity and character of these noble persons'. They too were allowed to take all their possessions with them. The Roman Catholic religion was to be maintained and the monasteries preserved;

and the Bishop of Cuba was to continue to enjoy his privileges, except that his appointment of priests had first to be approved by the British Governor. The inhabitants of Havana were allowed to keep their property in the town but, should it remain in British custody after peace was declared, they could opt out and leave the city within seven years.

The British however rejected three requests: the port of Havana was no longer to be neutral and at the service of Spain; the merchants of Cadiz were not to be given passports; and the free export of tobacco was refused. (Later, tobacco and sugar were sold in England for £700,000.)

The twenty-three points of capitulation having been agreed to, the document was signed on 12 August 1762. The signatures read: 'G. POCOCK, ALBEMARLE, EL MARQUES DEL REAL TRANSPORTE, JUAN DE PRADO'.

In accordance with their Sovereign's decree, the time had now come to put into effect the terms of the document signed by Sir George Pocock and Lord Albemarle on 5 June 1762, aiming at an equal distribution of 'plunder and booty' between sea and land forces, should the Havana campaign succeed.

Between the Commanders-in-Chief, a third ('five-fifteenths') of the whole was to be equally divided: this meant that Sir George Pocock and Lord Albemarle each now received £122,697. 10s. 1d. The seconds-in-command, Commodore the Hon. Augustus Keppel and Lieutenant-General George Eliott (relegated, through no fault of his, to an inconspicuous role at Guanabacoa) each received £24,539. 10s. 1d. ('nine-fifteenths' is given in the original script). The balance was distributed down the scale between captains, officers, seamen and marines; and officers and soldiers of the land forces. As Lord Albemarle and his two brothers all held important commands, it was said by the malicious that the expedition had been undertaken 'solely to put money in the Keppels' pockets'. Major-General William Keppel's share of the booty is not specified, but as such distributions were always loaded in favour of the senior officers, this one presumably followed the practice of the time; though the distribution at bottom level was certainly iniquitous. Of those bluejackets and private soldiers to whose 'patriotic endeavours' Mante had declared that Sir George Pocock and Lord Albemarle 'owed their success', the bluejacket's 'booty' was £3. 14s. 9¾d.; and the private soldier's equivalent was £4. 1s. 8½d.

There were also complaints from outside the immediate orbit of Havana about the distribution of prize-money. Sir James Douglas petitioned unsuccessfully for a share in it. And after the war Major-General Phineas Lyman, commanding the American provincials at Havana, petitioned the British Government for land grants in the south-west provinces of America, as his army's share of prize-money earned in the campaign. The resistance of the British Crown kindled further resentment. This may have been a factor in the rebellion of the American colonies ten years later.

As Major-General Keppel now succumbed to the prevailing fever, his second-in-command (the name was left blank in Keppel's journal) took possession of the North Gate on 14 August. At the same time, Captain Duncan in the *Valiant* took possession of the men-of-war in the harbour. These consisted of nine ships, five of seventy guns: *El Tigre*, *El Infante*, *El Soverano*, *La Reynha* and *El Aquilon*; and four '60s': *L'America*, *El Conquistador*, *El Santo Antonia* and *El San Jenero*. In addition to these, the Spaniards lost the three ships sunk across the boom (a '70' and two '60s'); two ships taken by the *Alarm*, and another taken by the *Defiance*: and two ships on the stocks (one an '80' and the other a '60') which were destroyed by order of Captain Duncan. A fifth of the whole Spanish fleet was captured by the British at Havana. In addition were 'half-a-dozen royal frigates and despatch vessels captured either in the port or outside...a ship of seventy-eight guns and six more frigates belonging to the great trading corporations, and nearly a hundred merchant-men. The booty was further swelled by over a hundred brass guns, quantities of warlike stores, and an immense amount of merchandise.' This total was subsequently valued at three million pounds sterling. As soon as 'formal possession of the Havannah' had been taken, on 16 August, Commodore Keppel in the *Valiant* sailed into the harbour, heading His Britannic Majesty's victorious fleet.

Compared to this stupendous prize, the toll of British dead and wounded seemed small. Only about 560 men were killed or died of wounds. But 4,708 servicemen perished from sickness, and nearly all the remainder, both in England and America, including Lord Albemarle and Commodore Keppel themselves, suffered crippling ill-health for the rest of their lives.

I I

Aftermath

Sir George Pocock's letter of 9 October to the Board of Admiralty reported that, two months after the British victory, conditions were still far from satisfactory. Fresh food was still lamentably short and the prevailing sickness continued on a diet of mainly 'salt provisions'; and 'the extraordinary expense of medicines' made the doctors' tasks 'doubly difficult'. The 'unhealthy season' had taken appalling toll of life in both services, though now Sir George hoped that the cooler weather would relieve the men's suffering. And, 'as all the ships, except three of the line' were due to depart within the month, the sea air should benefit all on board.

The Admiral confirmed that already, on 14 September, he had ordered Commodore Keppel to make ready for sea the *Valiant, Orford, Téméraire, Edgar, Alcide, Nottingham, Pembroke, Trent* and *Richmond*, and he expected him now to sail 'in a day or two'. Following previous instructions received from the Board of Admiralty, Sir George was then directing the Commodore to proceed to Port Royal, there to take command of the Jamaica station.

The *Belleisle, Ripon, Hampton Court,* and *Thunder* and *Granada* bomb-vessels were to remain at Havana, together with eight transports, three hospital ships and two ordnance ships. Forty sail of transports had been allotted to take on board the regulars and provincials destined for North America, who were to be conveyed by the *Intrepid*, due to sail that month. But, owing to the bad health of the army (as

Lord Albemarle had already stressed to Lord Egremont on
21 August) Lord Albemarle was afraid he could only send
the provincials, as his regular troops were too ill to travel. Sir
George himself proposed sailing for England on 20 October,
taking with him the *Namur, Culloden, Marlborough, Devonshire*,
and *Temple*; the Spanish ship of the line *El Infante*, the prizes
San Jenaro and *Asuncion*; forty-nine sail of transports, three
bomb tenders, and the storeship *Admiral Pocock*.

The *Sutherland* and *Dover* had already sailed on 20 August
with the transports for Spain, where subsequently they
landed the Spanish officers, seamen and soldiers. On return
to their native land, both Admiral Don Juan de Prado and
the Marques del Real Transporte were disgraced. But in
homage to the heroic memory of Captain Luis de Velasco,
the King decreed that henceforth the head of his family
should be ennobled, to become the Marques Fuerte del
Morro, and that in future, there should always be a ship of
the line in the Spanish fleet named *Velasco*.

Sir George Pocock reported on the sorry condition of the
British ships. As the *Stirling Castle* could hardly float, after
her stores and provisions had been taken out he sank her in
the upper reaches of Havana harbour. To replace her, he
put the *Infante* (of seventy guns) into commission and ordered
the *Stirling Castle*'s captain, officers and company to take her
over, giving the officers commissions and warrants—which
action he hoped 'their Lordships' would approve. Despite
the repairs she had received at Portsmouth after the Belleisle campaign, Commodore Keppel's ship, *Valiant*, had a bad
leak. She was to be careened on reaching Jamaica; and
Marlborough, Temple, Culloden and *Intrepid* were also leaking
badly. But Sir George reported that the *San Jenaro* (a Spanish
prize-ship of sixty guns) was a new ship, which he considered
'very fit for His Majesty's service'. He added that Havana
had 'a very good careening wharf and accommodations for

that purpose'. As part of his squadron would have to remain behind 'for the protection of the Havana and its dependencies', Sir George had found it vitally necessary to appoint persons to act as storekeeper, master-attendant and builder; and he reported that he had appointed three officers from his flagship, *Namur*, to take on these duties.

The civil administration was to remain as it was, carried out by *alcades, corregidors* and 'inferior officers', and according to Sir George 'everywhere' seemed 'very quiet and easy'. On hearing of the surrender of Havana, the officer in command at the Matanzas had blown up the fort, and the inhabitants had submitted 'readily' to the British officers in command who, with some 300 troops, had been sent there by direction of himself and Lord Albemarle.

Finally, Sir George reported that Lord Albemarle proposed to return home towards the end of December and had asked for a ship of the line to convey him with his retinue. The *Ripon* had been made ready for this purpose.

In his despatch Admiral Pocock was generous in his praise of Commodore Keppel's competence, declaring:

> I am glad on this occasion to do justice to the distinguished merit of Commodore Keppel, who executed the service under his directions, on the Coximar side, with the greatest spirit, activity, and diligence.

In accordance with Lord Anson's original instructions, the Commodore was now to take over command from Sir George Pocock himself, and Sir George was to return home.

On 22 October Admiral Pocock made an abortive attempt, in bad weather, to leave Havana, resulting in the loss of three ships 'and the whole fleet being in the utmost danger'. On 3 November he set sail again, this time with five ships of the line, *Namur, Culloden, Marlborough, Devonshire* and *Temple*; several prizes; about fifty transports and the storeship

Admiral Pocock. He fared no better. For about three weeks his squadron had a fine passage; then 'within 200 leagues of the Land's End', it ran into a gale from the east and was driven off course. As many of the ships were leaky they were unable either to make for land or keep to sea. The *Marlborough* bore away for Lisbon, but just as she was about to founder, providentially she was rescued by the *Antelope* from Newfoundland. The *Devonshire* and *Temple* went to the bottom; the *Culloden* suffered 'the utmost distress', and twelve of the transports foundered with all hands. Having already suffered untold hardships in the Havana campaign, the crews of the remaining ships afloat suffered further agonies of thirst, sickness and fatigue, and more than half of them died. The *Namur* herself, with Sir George Pocock on board, did not reach Portsmouth till 13 January 1763.

He got no further command.

Two of Lord Albemarle's engineers must be accounted for before closing the epic engagement of Havana: Colonel Patrick Mackellar, architect of the siege; and that enigmatic historian, Thomas Mante, who had added so much to the vivid portrayal of the campaign.

Concerning Mackellar, very little can be gleaned from contemporary *Lists of Officers of the Royal Engineers (1660–1898).* But he was Chief Engineer at Minorca at the time of his death there in November 1778. The *Gentleman's Magazine* adds the melancholy fact that he never recovered from the wounds he sustained at Havana. A hard-working, efficient, brave man.

According to his own account, Mante after Havana accompanied the American contingent back to Florida, and served as 'major of brigade' to Colonel Dudley Bradstreet against the Indians in 1764. But his name does not appear in any British *Army List*, nor in Porter's *History of the Royal*

Engineers. His biographer, Frank Managhan, identifies him as 'Junius' (that anonymous critic of George III and his ministers), and thinks he may have been a double agent for England and France. Certainly his knowledge of the French language and his subsequent skill in translating the works of French war tacticians gives credence to this view. Mante's account of the storming of El Morro is so graphic that he must have been a participant; and Augustus Keppel's biographer, his great-nephew Thomas Keppel, is so convinced of its authenticity that he gives it 'verbatim' coverage in his *Life of Admiral Keppel*. (He always writes 'Mante' without the 'e'.) Furthermore, Mante's subsequent publications received wide publicity, particularly in America. And his translation of *A System of Tactics* from the French of Joly de Maizeray was dedicated to the hero of the Cabaña heights, Brigadier Guy Carleton (afterwards Lord Dorchester), presumably with his authority.

Directly he had taken possession of Havana harbour, Keppel began to refit and prepare his squadron for sea. He continued to feel uneasy about the leaky state of his own ship, *Valiant*, reporting to the Admiralty (as Sir George Pocock had done) that her condition was becoming 'more and more unpleasant, and unfit for this hot climate. Her leak rather increases than lessens, and the constant pumping of her has already had its bad effect among a feeble and sickly ship's company.' He stated that he would have her careened directly she reached Jamaica, but he had to admit that she had been 'a leaky ship ever since she was built'. He was afraid *Valiant*'s condition made her unfit to be a cruiser—which he deplored, as he really thought she was without comparison 'the finest ship I ever was in'.

Despite this the Commodore put to sea on 12 October with a squadron of seven ships of the line and several frigates.

He despatched one battleship and two frigates to cruise off Cap François on the look-out for Admiral Blénac's French fleet. Instead of meeting any of the enemy's ships of the line, the three British ships fell in with three French frigates, *Étourdi*, *Expédition* and *Velouté*, convoying eight or ten merchant vessels bound for France. To these they gave chase and, with the *Valiant* arriving at the crucial moment, they were fortunate in capturing most of the convoy. The *Étourdi* and two or three small merchantmen outsailed the foul British ships, but as the captured vessels were laden with cargoes of sugar, coffee and indigo, they proved a rich prize.

On 3 November Commodore Keppel and his squadron arrived at Port Royal, Jamaica, by which time the *Valiant* was leaking so badly that she was barely above water. Even so, the short sea-passage had had a beneficial effect on the squadron crews, and as it was the Commodore's purpose to keep all his 'effective' ships constantly cruising, not only did the health of his men improve but the ships' actions 'cleared the sea of the enemy's privateers' and brought many more prizes, both French and Spanish, into the harbour of Port Royal.

Early in January 1763 Keppel received two important communications. One announced that preliminaries for peace between England and France had been signed as far back as 3 November 1762. The other, dated 9 November 1762, from John Cleveland, Board of Admiralty, told him that George III had sanctioned his promotion to rear-admiral of the Blue—and this at the age of only thirty-seven. (Rodney was the youngest ever to be so promoted; then Keppel; and then Nelson, at the age of thirty-nine.)

As Admiral Keppel's health had been permanently undermined, when a cessation of hostilities was ordered he applied to the Admiralty for permission to relinquish his command and to return to England. His application was granted, but so many matters still needed his attention that he was unable to leave Port Royal for another year.

In January 1764 Sir William Barnaby arrived to take over command of the Jamaica station, and in March Admiral Keppel set sail for England. But he had been hardly a week at sea before the leak in the *Valiant* became so serious that he had to suffer the mortification of returning to Port Royal, to have her careened again. On 8 May he set sail once more and, despite the ship's parlous condition and a very sick crew, he arrived back intact in England on 26 June.

By this time England had been at peace for over a year, and the Seven Years' War was an event of the past.

12

The Final Irony

Lord Albemarle took over the Governorship of Havana until such time as he could hand it over to his brother, Major-General William Keppel. When reporting to Lord Egremont on 21 August 1762 he had emphasised that the general health of his troops was still very bad. For this reason, he had been unable to go to the assistance of Major-General Amherst in America, who had suddenly informed him that he depended 'entirely' upon his sending him 'eight thousand men of his Expedition against the Louisianne', and also desiring him and Sir George Pocock 'to fix His Rendezvous and the time for his joining the Troops'. Lord Albemarle had justifiably complained that until that moment he had had no idea that, subsequent to Havana, Louisiana was to be attacked 'by the Mouth of the River Mississippi' and had stressed again that his army was 'by no means fit for immediate or severe service'. So he had regretted that at that moment he was unable to send back the troops 'under the command of Brigadier Burton' until he could estimate how many men he would need to garrison the forts of Havana and that part of Cuba surrounding them.

On 7 October he was no more sanguine when he reported to Lord Egremont that 'our Sickness instead of diminishing increases dayly notwithstanding the Great Care and attention that is paid to the Sick.' Since the capitulation 3,000 men had died and many in hospital were unlikely to recover. A sick man himself, Lord Albemarle took a morbid view of the general scene: 'I have Scarce a Relief for the necessary

Guards of the Garrison and in many Parts of the Country the Militia and Peasants are still in arms for want of Troops showing themselves amongst them.'

He felt that Havana and its environs should never be left without at least 4,000 troops 'able to bear arms' as 'in this unhealthy Climate you may always reckon upon One Third of your Force sick or unfit for Service.' He recommended that 6,000 men should be left under the command of the Governor, but hoped that somehow he could return 'all the Provincials and independants' to North America by the middle of the month in which he wrote.

As Governor, Lord Albemarle had a difficult time adjudicating, trying to preserve his authority and impartiality, for he was not a patient man. First, the Governor of Santiago declared himself Governor and Captain-General of the island of Cuba, and enlisted a lot of local support for his view. Lord Albemarle commanded the leading magistrates to appear before him, but admitted to Lord Egremont that, if they refused, he would have to depend on reliable weather and better health in his troops before he could send army detachments to enforce his orders.

Secondly, the Bishop of Cuba refused point-blank to furnish Lord Albemarle with a list of the 'Ecclesiasticks in his Diocese', whereby Lord Albemarle had been ordered to judge the individual merits of those priests recommended for preferment. And the Bishop threatened 'in an illegal and imperious Manner to Complain to the Courts of Great Britain and Spain of the Irregularity as a Breach of the Capitulation...', still considering himself a subject of 'His Catholic Majesty', and not of the sovereign head of a conquering state. Lord Albemarle's answer to this insubordination was to deport the Bishop to Florida in a British man-of-war, in order to restore 'harmony and good understanding to the town of Havana'.

Lastly, he levied dubious taxes on both British and American traders. The British Government said that he had no right to do this, and that he was expected to reimburse the money to the traders concerned.

But before he ceded office to his brother, Lord Albemarle received a letter from his royal patron, the Duke of Cumberland, which acted as a panacea to his sense of outrage. It was written from Windsor Great Lodge on 2 October:

> My dear Albemarle—
> You have made me the happiest man existing, nay, you have almost repaid me for the severe anxieties I have gone through for the last three months...and I strut and plume myself...as if it was I that had taken the Havannah. In short, you have done your King and country the most materiall service that any man has ever done since we were a country, and you have shewn yourself an excellent officer; all of which I knew was in you, but now the whole world see it and own it. Millitarily speaking, I take your siege to have been the most difficult that has been since the invention of artillery.

The Duke complimented 'both the brothers', and declared: 'The storm of the Moro does William's heart and hedd [*sic*] great honour.' He then went on to give some pertinent details of the effect of the capture of Havana on leading politicians at home.

> I am sorry to say the Minister [Lord Bute] is not quite so much obliged to you, for you have removed the peace.... You may judge the part I take when I tell you Permis* is once a fortnight for four hours at least in the

*The Duke of Newcastle's nickname because of his diffidence in approaching a royal princess.

library here, you will see too much of all this at your
return.

The Duke assured Lord Albemarle that the King seemed 'to
allow you and familly the merit you and they deserve';
and ended by hoping that 'we make you as rich as Creses.'

As the new Governor of Havana, William Keppel's task was
to restore to Spain 'all the Territory' which the British forces
had captured during their three months' campaign, and all
the fortresses and 'the Artillery and Ammunition which were
found there, at the time of the Conquest'. (This was instructed by Lord Egremont in a letter dated 16 March 1763.)
    Luckily for Augustus Keppel, the Lords of Admiralty
acted more quickly, anticipating the peace. In a secret
despatch to Lord Albemarle dated 2 February 1763, Lord
Egremont had included a copy of their Lordships' urgent
instructions to the Admiral at Jamaica. They had ordered
him to make sure that all the Spanish ships in Havana harbour (as already enumerated by Sir George Pocock) were
to be fitted and sent immediately to Jamaica, Halifax or
England, with all the 'stores proper' to be put on British
ships bound for home. The Admiral was also told to destroy all Spanish ships, notably the *America*, if unfit for
service, having first removed from them 'whatever may be
serviceable'.

Throughout the gruelling campaign at Havana, George III's
Ministers had sued for peace with France. Although paying
lip-service to the general rejoicing occasioned by Captain
Hervey's return to England with news of the victory, Lord
Bute and his plenipotentiary, the Duke of Bedford, re-
doubled their efforts to achieve peace. On 13 October 1762
Lord Bute wrote complainingly to the Duke:

The taking of Havana has turned the heads of the wisest men and those most inclined to peace: men that your Grace is well acquainted with, and whose voice you have heard in the Cabinet loudest for almost any peace, now think the French terms ought to be screwed up tighter.

With the bells of victory ringing in their ears and the smoke of the celebration bonfires filling their nostrils, both Grenville and Lord Egremont declared that they would sign 'no such peace as Bute desired'. Behind them rose the clamour, particularly from the City, that Spain must first denounce the 'Family Compact' before any move for peace was made. Unpopular as he knew himself to be, Lord Bute did not dare face Parliament, or even the Cabinet, with his present plans. On his own initiative, he revoked the Duke of Bedford's plenary powers and told him to expect a 'New Project of Peace', as England's last word.

As Grenville was now pressing to bring back the Duke of Newcastle and his friends to Council, Bute began manoeuvring behind the scenes to oust Grenville from the Foreign Office and as leader of the House of Commons. Despite his allegiance to Bute, Lord Halifax was in favour of a coalition with the Duke of Newcastle and was prepared to act as go-between; and even the King sanctioned an overture to the Duke. But, though it was made, Newcastle refused to play, and by so doing he made things easier for Bute who now determined to seek the help of Henry Fox. During his recent term of office as Paymaster, Fox's blatant appropriation of public funds had gained him the opprobrium of most of his colleagues, but his toughness and tenacity in achieving his objective were qualities Bute now needed. He persuaded Fox to accept the leadership of the Commons 'without office but with almost despotic powers'. Grenville was then forced to go to the Admiralty and Halifax became Secretary of State for the North.

In principle, it was decided that the 'New Project' should stick to the English plan in Europe of a general evacuation of Germany and Portugal, while, in North America and the West Indies, Florida or Puerto Rico should be demanded for Havana. Lord Bute revealed the terms secretly to the Comte de Viri, Sardinian Ambassador in London (who was his intermediary with Paris), and told him that on no account was the Duke of Bedford or the Marques de Grimaldi, the Spanish Ambassador at Paris, to be told of them.

This time the Court of France needed no preparation as, with all the implications before him of the British victory at Havana, the pragmatic Foreign Secretary, the Duc de Choiseul, had decided that enough was enough. Havana, he said, 'had stopped Grimaldi's cackle', and he set out to force the English terms down Spain's throat. But he was too much of a realist not to see that to achieve peace quickly France too must make some major concessions.

On 22 and 23 October Bute's reconstructed Cabinet met to discuss the draft of the 'New Project' which was passed unanimously, as it stood. By the end of the week it was in Paris. To quote: 'Hard as the terms were, Choiseul ... did not flinch.' If Spain would relinquish Florida, she was offered that part of Louisiana which was not already promised to England; and she accepted this. As a result, the Preliminaries of Peace were signed at Fontainebleau on 3 November.

There was still a snag, as the Duke of Bedford had failed to include an article whereby, in the Prussian Rhineland, France was to evacuate Cleves, Wesel and Gueldres. By omitting to do so, Frederick of Prussia (who already suspected Bute and Bedford of the most dubious methods) was convinced they had tricked him again. He sent a furious protest to London, where the Preliminaries had still to be submitted to Parliament, before a definitive treaty could be made. When the terms leaked out 'the anger of the nation blazed'. The King insulted the Duke of Devonshire, thereby alienating many of his associates; and Pitt and the Duke of Newcastle took to meeting in the Duke of Cumberland's house (as the latter had already told Lord Albemarle). But Bute had picked the right man to do his work for him, and by the time Parliament met on 9 December, Fox had cajoled, bribed and blackmailed members of both Houses into a state of sullen acquiescence.

In the House of Lords Lord Hardwicke tore the peace to tatters; in the Commons Pitt (who had risen from a bed of sickness for the occasion) denounced the peace for three-and-a-half hours. All to no avail. Fox had done his work. In the Lords the peace was agreed to without a division; in the Commons it was carried by an overwhelming majority.

On 10 February 1763 the definitive treaty was signed at Paris by the Duke of Bedford, the Duc de Choiseul and the Marques de Grimaldi, with the 'Family Compact' left in being. As agreed, Spain gave up all her North American possessions east of the Mississippi, then known as Florida, to England.

Finally, having acquired immense booty at Havana, albeit at an appalling cost of human suffering, and having reduced the Spanish fleet to impotence, six months after her decisive victory England handed Havana back to Spain.

Appendix: Lord Albemarle's Will

On 13 February 1762, 'being shortly to proceed beyond sea...', George Lord Albemarle made a will. In it he left an annuity of £200 a year for life to Mrs Sarah Stanley 'of the parish of St. George, Hanover Square', his devoted mistress over the past ten years; and he provided for his daughter by her (also Sarah), 'aged 9 years in May next', leaving her an annuity of £100 until the age of twenty-one or until she married, to be used for her education and maintenance 'in such manner as my honoured mother Anne Countess of Albemarle shall see fit'. Thereafter, on her coming of age or getting married she was to inherit a further £5,000, also subject to Lady Albemarle's approval, if living, or, if she were dead, then with the approval of two of the trustees, General James Cholmondeley and General Studholme Hodgson.

To his brother Augustus Keppel 'in case Augustus shall sail with me and shall survive me', Lord Albemarle left the residue of his estate, and appointed him executor of his will. To Augustus's care he left his male child by Sarah Stanley, christened George Stanley in the parish of St. George, Hanover Square, who was to reach the age of eight 'in September next'. His education and maintenance were to be supervised by Augustus, and the boy too was to receive an annuity of £100 a year. Should he die, his annuity was to be transferred to the children of Lord Albemarle's sister, Lady Caroline Adair.

Lord Albemarle's plate, family pictures and personal possessions were to go to the successor of the title, but should his younger brother Henry succeed, he was specifically excluded from acquiring any of these benefits.

Finally, Lord Albemarle appointed a third trustee to his will: Joshua Stampe of Lincoln's Inn (Solicitor).

Glossary & Bibliography

Glossary of Military and Naval Terms

abatis   Improvised obstacle of trees felled with branches towards enemy.

bastion   Projecting work on line of fortifications, usually with two faces towards enemy and two flanks from which defenders' weapons can cover neighbouring *curtains* and next bastions' faces.

battery   (1) Platform or fortified work where artillery is mounted. (2) One gun, or several working together.

bomb   Hollow iron sphere filled with explosive (now called a shell): hence *bombard, bomb-ship*.

bower-anchor   Two large anchors borne at ship's bows.

boyau   (1) Small gallery of a *mine*. (2) Zig-zag branch of siege trench, sometimes leading to magazine.

breastwork   Temporary defensive mound a few feet high, used in the field.

cable's length   About 200 yards.

careen   Clean, caulk or repair a ship which has been laid on one side.

casement or *casemate*   Bomb-proof structure in fortifications, either from which weapons can be fired, or to give shelter to garrison.

cay   Islet, reef or bank, especially in Caribbean.

coehorn   Small mortar firing grenades.

counterscarp   Outer wall or slope of *ditch* (contrast *escarpment*).

courtin or *curtain*   Main wall of fortification, lying between *bastions*, towers or gates.

covert-way or *covered-way*   Infantry position at top of *counterscarp*, with *parapet* giving cover to defenders who can fire over it down *glacis*.

ditch   Large trench (fosse) to form obstacle in front of fortification (at El Morro, 50–100 feet wide and 45–65 feet deep). Sometimes filled with water.

embrasure   Opening in *parapet* through which a gun can fire.

escarpment or *scarp*   Inner wall or slope of *ditch*, or front face of *rampart* (contrast *counterscarp*).

fascine   Firmly bound cylindrical faggot of brushwood for filling *ditches* in an attack, or constructing *batteries* or other works. Typically 10 feet by 9 inches.

foul Ship's bottom encrusted with seaweed, barnacles, etc.

gabion Cylindrical wicker basket, for filling with earth when improvising fortifications. Typically 3 feet high by 2 feet diameter.

glacis Long cleared smooth slope running down towards enemy from *covered-way* or crest of *counterscarp*, swept by fire from *ramparts*.

grounding-out Laying a ship aground for examination or repair.

kedge To move a ship (*e.g.* when aground) by hauling on hawser attached to small kedge-anchor dropped some distance away.

mantelet or *mantlet* Screen of metal or rope-work to protect a gun in an *embrasure* or *casemate*, or the attackers of a fort.

merlon Raised part of *parapet* between two *embrasures*, sometimes pierced by a gun-loop.

mine Tunnel dug by attackers: generally used to place explosives to blow up part of work being attacked. (The defenders might use counter-mines.)

mortar Short-barrelled large-calibre artillery, firing high-trajectory projectiles (usually explosive) over a shorter range than guns.

parapet Earth bank or stone wall to give troops observation and cover from fire.

rampart Large bank forming main portion of fortifications, usually with a parapet and wide enough to mount guns.

redan Projecting work on line of fortifications, with two faces in a V-shape: it has no flanks (contrast *bastion*). Mostly used in defensive works.

redoubt Small enclosed work usually outside line of fortifications: a chain of redoubts can form a mutually supporting ring.

royal Mortar of $5\frac{1}{2}$-inch bore and range about 600 yards.

sap Trench dug forward towards besieged place by *sappers* working in and protected by it. Usually constructed in zig-zags.

stream-anchor Anchor intermediate in size between *bower-anchor* and *kedge-anchor*, used when mooring ship in sheltered position.

Bibliography

MANUSCRIPT SOURCES

British Library

Newcastle, 1st Duke of, 'Official Correspondence', British Library Additional MSS.: 32920 (1761); 32948–52 & 54 (1763); 32955, 32959, 32961–3 (1764); 32965–71 (1765); 32973 (1766); Hardwicke Papers: 35870 (1760); 36122 (1748)

National Maritime Museum, London

Keppel Papers (Post Mortem on Lord Albemarle)

Public Record Office

Albemarle, George, 3rd Earl of, Will, 1770
Calendar of Home Office Papers—Army Commissions: 741 (1762); 819 (8 Mar 1763); 821/2 (11 Mar 1763); 830 (19 Mar 1763); 1109 (8 Dec 1763); 1110 (10 Dec 1763); 1113 (11/12 Dec 1763)

PUBLISHED SOURCES

Albemarle, George Thomas, 6th Earl of, *Memoirs of the Marquess of Rockingham*, 2 vols., Richard Bentley, London, 1852
——, *Fifty Years of My Life*, 2 vols., Macmillan, 1876
Ayling, Stanley, *The Elder Pitt, Earl of Chatham*, Collins, 1976
Callender, Sir Geoffrey, *Sea Kings of Britain*, vol. 3 (Keppel to Nelson, 1760–1805), Longmans, 1939
Clowes, Sir William Laird, *The Royal Navy, A History*, vol. 3 [of 7] (Expedition to Belleisle), Sampson Low, 1898
Cokayne, G. E. & Gibbs, Hon. Vicary (edd), *The Complete Peerage*, vol. 3 (Cumberland), St Catherine Press, London, 2nd edn. 1910
Corbett, Sir Julian, *England in the Seven Years' War*, 2 vols., Longmans, 1907
—— (ed), *Signals and Instructions, 1776–94*, Navy Records Society, vol. 35, London, 1908

Cuba, Publicaciones del Archivo Nacional de, vol. 18 (*La Toma de la Havana en 1762*), Havana, 1948

Dictionary of National Biography (Keppel), Smith Elder, 1908

Fortescue, Hon. Sir John, *A History of the British Army*, vols. 1 & 2 [of 13], Macmillan, 2nd edn. 1910

—— (ed), *Correspondence of King George III, 1760–83*, vol. 1 [of 6], Macmillan, 1927

Green, Lt-Col. Howard, *Famous Engagements*, vol. 2 (Culloden), London, 1971

Hart, Francis Russell, *The Siege of Havana, 1762*, Houghton Mifflin, Boston, 1931

—— *Spanish Documents Relating to the Siege of Havana*, Proceedings of Massachusetts Hist. Soc., Boston, 1932

Holbrooke, Lieut. Bernard, *The Siege and Capture of Belleisle*, Journal of Royal United Services Institute, London, vol. 43, 1899

Keppel, Hon. & Rev. Thomas, *The Life of Augustus, Viscount Keppel*, 2 vols., Henry Colburn, London, 1842

Laughton, Sir John Knox, *From Howard to Nelson, Twelve Sailors*, Lawrence & Bullen, London, 1899

Mahan, Capt. Alfred Thayer, U.S.N., *The Influence of Sea Power upon History*, Sampson Low, 1889

Mante, Thomas, *The History of the Late War in North America and the Islands of the West Indies*, Strachan & Cadell, London, 1772

Marcus, Geoffrey Jules, *Quiberon Bay, the Campaign in Home Waters, 1759*, Hollis & Carter, 1960

Plumb, John Harold, *Chatham*, Collins, 1953

Syrett, David, *The Siege and Capture of Havana, 1762*, Navy Records Society, vol. 114, London, 1970

Thomas, Hugh, *Cuba, The Pursuit of Freedom*, Eyre & Spottiswoode, 1971

Toynbee, Mrs Paget (ed), *Letters of Horace Walpole*, vols. 8–13 [of 16], Clarendon Press, 1903

Tunstall, Brian, *William Pitt, Earl of Chatham*, Hodder & Stoughton, 1938

Watson, J. Steven, *The Reign of George III, 1760–1815*, Clarendon Press, 1960

Williams, Basil, *The Whig Supremacy, 1714–60* (Appendix, Lists of Holders of Various Offices), Clarendon Press, 1962

Young, Peter & Adair, John, *Hastings to Culloden*, Bell, 1964

Biographical Index

Biographical Index

THE KEPPELS

Albemarle (William Anne Keppel), 2nd Earl of, Lieutenant-General (1702–54)
Named after his godmother Queen Anne, he succeeded his father in 1718, and five years later married Lady Anne Lennox, daughter of the first Duke of Richmond. Out of their fifteen offspring, five sons survived infancy. The five surviving sons were:

Albemarle (George Keppel), 3rd Earl of, Lieutenant-General (1724–72)
Educated at Westminster. Appointed ensign in the Coldstream Guards in 1738, he became Cumberland's favourite ADC, and was with him at Fontenoy (1745) and Culloden (1746)—where he was lucky to escape death when a Highlander fired at him point-blank believing him to be the Duke. Subsequently ADC to George II, he sat in the House of Commons for some years before his succession to the earldom in 1754. By 1760 he was a lieutenant-general, privy councillor and Governor of Jersey. In 1762, through Cumberland's influence, he took command of the expedition to Havana. On his triumphant return (with his £120,000 share of the prize-money) he was nominated Knight of the Bath (1764), and the Garter followed in 1771. Alleged to be a harsh and exacting conqueror.

Keppel, Hon. Augustus, 1st Viscount Keppel, Admiral of the Blue (1725–86)
Educated at Westminster, he entered the navy in 1735, serving as lieutenant in *Centurion* during Anson's celebrated voyage round the world, 1741–44. Three years later, the 50-gun ship *Maidstone*, under his command, ran aground in the Bay of Biscay while chasing the enemy, and was wrecked. At the consequent court-martial Keppel was honourably acquitted. He sat on Byng's court-martial in 1757 and vainly endeavoured to secure the merciful intervention of Parliament. In 1761, as captain of *Valiant*, he commanded a squadron cooperating with the army at the reduction of Belleisle, and soon afterwards was appointed commodore and second-in-command to Pocock for the Havana expedition. In the early 1770s he became much involved in political intrigue and saw little active service, but in 1778, in anticipation of a French war, he was promoted admiral of the Blue and commander-in-chief of the Grand Fleet. Through

unremitting exertion, he galvanised a lethargic navy into some state of readiness. Next year he engaged the French fleet inconclusively off Brest: for which, following much political backbiting, he was belatedly court-martialled for neglect of duty. The charge was pronounced 'malicious and ill-founded' and he was once again honourably acquitted. As a member of Parliament he lost no opportunity of criticising the conduct of naval affairs while Sandwich was First Lord of the Admiralty. After the fall of North's administration, Keppel was himself appointed First Lord and raised to the peerage as a viscount, but soon afterwards his health finally broke down and he retired from public life.

Keppel, Hon. William, Lieutenant-General (1727–82) Educated at West-minster (where he was known as 'Fat Van'), became ensign in 2nd Foot Guards 1744. In Flanders as ADC to Sir John Ligonier, he was wounded and taken prisoner at the Battle of Laffeldt in 1747. Captain in 1st Foot Guards 1750, and second major (with rank of colonel) 1760; colonel of 56th Foot 1761. Divisional general to Havana campaign (major-general), he was appointed lieutenant-general and commander-in-chief Ireland 1763. A member of Parliament from 1776, he died unmarried.

Keppel, Hon. Frederick, Bishop of Exeter (1728–77) Educated at Westminster and Christ Church, Oxford, he won rapid preferment after his ordination, becoming chaplain to George II and III, and a canon of Windsor from 1754 until 1762, when he was consecrated Bishop of Exeter. Three years later he was appointed Dean of Windsor and Registrar of the Garter. A jovial man with homely features who enjoyed good living.

Keppel, Hon. Henry (born 1741) Youngest of the five, he vanished from the records after running into debt in Gibraltar and surrendering to the Spanish Governor. Described in a contemporary source as being 'a captain in the army'.

OTHERS MENTIONED

Amherst, Sir Jeffery, later 1st Baron Amherst (1717–97) His rapid promotion in the army may indeed have been due to his early service on the staff of General Ligonier and the Duke of Cumberland; but Pitt recognised his qualities and in 1758 gave him command of the expedition to conquer French North America. After the fall of Ticonderoga, Quebec and Montreal in 1760 he received a knighthood and was appointed Governor-General of British North America. He was not very successful in his efforts to subdue the Indians there, despite his plan to use smallpox and bloodhounds as weapons against them. A soldier of unflinching determination, he was commander-in-chief of the forces on and off for some twenty years, being appointed field-marshal at the age of seventy-nine. He refused an earldom.

Anson, George, 1st Baron (1697–1762) Had many successes as a young naval officer, rising as commodore to command a squadron in the Pacific. In 1744 he continued westward round the world to reach London with a vast amount of plunder seized from the Spanish. Three years later he defeated the French fleet off Finnesterre and was raised to the peerage. His marriage to Lady Elizabeth Yorke brought him influence as well as wealth, and he spent the next few years reorganising the navy, especially the administration of the dockyards. A painstaking officer of sound judgement, he was advanced to admiral of the fleet in 1761, not long before he died at Moor Park, his country seat.

Cumberland, William Augustus, Duke of (1721–65) Third son of George II and Queen Caroline, he was educated for the navy, but his own tastes were military and he served with the army at Dettingen, in the Netherlands and at Culloden. First to be nominated Knight of the Bath when that order was revived in 1725, he was the founder of Ascot Races as well as Chancellor of the universities of St Andrews and Dublin. In Windsor Great Park, where he did much landscaping (including the excavation of Virginia Water), he is commemorated by Cumberland Lodge and the Obelisk, near the Savill Gardens. Appointed captain-general of the army in 1745, he did much to root out abuses and secure discipline and efficiency. A proud and unforgiving man, he enjoyed warfare for its own sake.

Douglas, Sir James, 1st Baronet (1703–87) Commanded *Mermaid* at the reduction of Louisbourg in 1744. Later he served under Knowles and was a member of the court-martial which in 1757 tried and condemned Admiral John Byng for neglect of duty. As commander-in-chief Leeward Islands, Douglas took Dominica from the French, and as Rodney's second-in-command seized Martinique. After reinforcing Pocock's fleet off Havana, he brought a convoy back to England, returning again as commander-in-chief West Indies. Advanced to full admiral in 1778, he saw no further service at sea. Created a baronet in 1786.

Eliott, George Augustus, later 1st Baron Heathfield of Gibraltar (1717–90) Educated at Leyden University, he trained at La Fère and saw service as a volunteer with the Prussian army in 1735. First commissioned as a field-engineer, he received rapid promotion, resigning as an engineer with the rank of lieutenant-colonel, thereafter making his regiment, the 1st Light Horse, a model for the rest of the army. He was most attentive to the welfare of his troopers and himself led a spartan life as vegetarian and teetotaller. In 1775 he was appointed Governor of Gibraltar, with instructions to prepare for a Spanish invasion, and four years later withstood a lengthy siege. He received a peerage on his return to England, three years before he died.

Elphinston, John (1722–85) A skilful and enterprising officer, he commanded the fireship *Salamander* under Howe at St Malo and Cherbourg in 1758, accompanied Saunders off Quebec, and bore Admiralty despatches to Rodney in the West Indies prior to the Havana operation. He subsequently led Pocock's fleet through the hazardous Old Bahama Channel and superintended transport during the siege. In 1769 he accepted a commission as rear-admiral in the Russian navy, leading their fleet to the destruction of some two hundred Turkish ships at Chesme Bay and being favourably received in St Petersburg by the Empress. Resuming his navy rank as captain, he served under Rodney at Grenada and off Martinique. His third son was created baronet, and it was his descendants who added the final 'e' to the family name.

Hervey, Augustus John, later 3rd Earl of Bristol (1724–79) Served with Byng in the Mediterranean in 1757 and gave evidence against him at the celebrated court-martial. Commanded the 74-gun *Dragon* under Augustus Keppel at Belleisle in 1760 and participated in Rodney's capture of Martinique and St Lucia from the French. He was sent back to England with despatches after the surrender of Havana, taking a valuable French prize en route. Turning from life at sea, he continued an MP until his succession to the earldom in 1775, besides holding positions at George III's court, the rank of vice-admiral of the Blue, and a seat on the Board of Admiralty. Hervey supported Augustus Keppel at the time of the latter's second court-martial, and it was his speech in 1779 which resulted in the removal of Sandwich as First Lord. A man totally without fear, though some considered him reckless and over-confident. He was buried at Ickworth, his country seat.

Knowles, Sir Charles, 1st Baronet (c1700–77) Reputed son of the 4th Earl of Banbury, his naval career contrasted strikingly with the customary pattern. Entering the service in 1718 as a captain's servant, he was rated able seaman in the Mediterranean 1721–26, and perhaps spent much of this commission educating himself—certainly his knowledge of mathematics and mechanics was far in advance of what was then usual in the navy. By 1730 he was a lieutenant and by 1741 fleet surveyor and engineer for an operation against New Granada (now Colombia). Two years later as commodore he was harrying Spanish settlements in Venezuela, and in 1747 was promoted rear-admiral of the White as commander-in-chief Jamaica. The next year his squadron closed with Spanish ships off Havana, but the inconclusive result was followed by courts-martial, and Knowles himself was reprimanded. Governor of Jamaica from 1752, he visited Havana as guest of the Spanish Governor and made careful mental note of its defences with a future invasion in mind. Knowles was Hawke's second-in-command for the abortive expedition against Rochefort in 1757, and after much public indignation he was relieved of his naval command and saw no further active service, though promoted full admiral in 1760 and created a baronet five years later. His character has been the subject of much contention: was he 'vain, foolish, grasping and tyrannical', or as another biographer wrote 'a man of spirit, ability and integrity'?

Mackellar, Patrick (1717-78) Trained as a military engineer at Woolwich, he saw much service overseas, and was severely wounded during Braddock's ill-fated campaign of 1754 in the Alleghanies. Two years later, as chief engineer for the frontier forts, he was taken prisoner by the French, and while confined in Quebec and Montreal learnt much about the defences of two cities he was later to assault. Wounded twice outside Quebec, in 1759 and 1760, he yet played a major part in all the subsequent operations which completed the conquest of Canada. Promoted lieutenant-colonel in 1762, he joined Albemarle's expedition to Havana, and his success in reducing El Morro (where once again he was wounded) earned him a high reputation. He died in 1778, 'full of zeal and energy', as Director of Engineers with the rank of full colonel. Many of the plans he drew are in the British Library.

Pocock, Sir George (1706-92) Entering the navy in 1718, he soon saw action at Cape Passaro, when with half their fleet destroyed the Spanish were forced to withdraw from Sicily. As rear-admiral of the White he was Watson's second-in-command in the East India station 1755-57, and on the latter's death succeeded him in the rank of vice-admiral. With his flag in *Yarmouth*, he fell in with the French East India Company's ships off Madras, and led the attack strictly in accordance with Admiralty 'Fighting Instructions'. The resulting action was inconclusive, and three of his captains were later found guilty by courts-martial. Pocock returned to England in 1761 and was promoted admiral of the Blue with a knighthood. In the following year he received his orders as naval commander-in-chief for the 'secret' expedition to Havana. After the Spanish surrender, he convoyed the transports and prizes home to England as a rich man. In 1766 he asked for his name to be struck off the list of admirals, some said from pique at the appointment of Saunders, his junior, as First Lord of the Admiralty.

Rodney, George Brydges, later 1st Baron Rodney (1719–92)   Educated for a short time at Harrow, he entered the navy as a king's letter boy in 1732. His first command, 1742, was *Plymouth*, in the rank of captain to which he had been promoted direct from lieutenant. In 1759, as rear-admiral with his flag in *Achilles*, he bombarded Havre and destroyed the boats and stores lying there ready for an invasion of England. Three years later, as commander-in-chief Leeward Islands, he took Martinique, St Lucia, Grenada and St Vincent, and on his return home was advanced to vice-admiral with a baronetcy. Never a rich man, his expenses fighting a parliamentary seat in 1768, coupled with considerable social extravagance, practically bankrupted him: indeed at one time he was forced to retreat abroad and live in Paris. In 1779, while making his way to command the Leeward Islands station for the second time, now in the rank of full admiral, he defeated a Spanish squadron off Cape St Vincent and relieved Gibraltar, then under siege. For this he was nominated an extra Knight of the Bath. With subsequent victories over the Dutch at St Eustatius and the French off Dominica also to his credit, Rodney was at last properly rewarded in 1782 with the thanks of Parliament, a peerage, and a pension of £2,000 a year to be settled on the title for ever.

Index

FLORIDA

HABANA
(CHAVANA)
CABAÑAS
GUANABACOA
Florida Strait
MATANZAS
Cay Sol
Bank

Great Bahama Bank

CUBA

Old Bahama Channel
Lobos Cay

YUCATAN

Yucatan Channel

G R E A T E R

SANTIAGO DE CUBA

JAMAICA
PORT ROYAL

HONDURAS

C A R I

Spanish

N

S

1000